INTRODUCING
ISSUES WITH
OPPOSING
VIEWPOINTS®

Water Resource Management

Patty Jo Sawvel, *Book Editor*

GREENHAVEN PRESS
A part of Gale, Cengage Learning

GALE
CENGAGE Learning™

Detroit • New York • San Francisco • New Haven, Conn • Waterville, Maine • London

Christine Nasso, *Publisher*
Elizabeth Des Chenes, *Managing Editor*

© 2008 Greenhaven Press, a part of Gale, Cengage Learning

Cover image copyright James N. Phelps, Jr, 2008. Used under license from Shutterstock.com.

ISBN: 978-0-7377-3979-4

Library of Congress Control Number: 2008926055

Printed in the United States of America
2 3 4 5 6 7 12 11 10 09 08

Contents

Chapter 3: Who Can Solve the Water Management Problem?

Foreword

Indulging in a wide spectrum of ideas, beliefs, and perspectives is a critical cornerstone of democracy. After all, it is often debates over differences of opinion, such as whether to legalize abortion, how to treat prisoners, or when to enact the death penalty, that shape our society and drive it forward. Such diversity of thought is frequently regarded as the hallmark of a healthy and civilized culture. As the Reverend Clifford Schutjer of the First Congregational Church in Mansfield, Ohio, declared in a 2001 sermon, "Surrounding oneself with only like-minded people, restricting what we listen to or read only to what we find agreeable is irresponsible. Refusing to entertain doubts once we make up our minds is a subtle but deadly form of arrogance." With this advice in mind, Introducing Issues with Opposing Viewpoints books aim to open readers' minds to the critically divergent views that comprise our world's most important debates.

Introducing Issues with Opposing Viewpoints simplifies for students the enormous and often overwhelming mass of material now available via print and electronic media. Collected in every volume is an array of opinions that captures the essence of a particular controversy or topic. Introducing Issues with Opposing Viewpoints books embody the spirit of nineteenth-century journalist Charles A. Dana's axiom: "Fight for your opinions, but do not believe that they contain the whole truth, or the only truth." Absorbing such contrasting opinions teaches students to analyze the strength of an argument and compare it to its opposition. From this process readers can inform and strengthen their own opinions, or be exposed to new information that will change their minds. Introducing Issues with Opposing Viewpoints is a mosaic of different voices. The authors are statesmen, pundits, academics, journalists, corporations, and ordinary people who have felt compelled to share their experiences and ideas in a public forum. Their words have been collected from newspapers, journals, books, speeches, interviews, and the Internet, the fastest growing body of opinionated material in the world.

Introducing Issues with Opposing Viewpoints shares many of the well-known features of its critically acclaimed parent series, Opposing Viewpoints. The articles are presented in a pro/con format, allowing readers to absorb divergent perspectives side by side. Active reading questions preface each viewpoint, requiring the student to approach the material thoughtfully and carefully. Useful charts, graphs, and cartoons supplement each article. A thorough introduction provides readers with crucial background on an issue. An annotated bibliography points the reader toward articles, books, and Web sites that contain additional information on the topic. An appendix of organizations to contact contains a wide variety of charities, nonprofit organizations, political groups, and private enterprises that each hold a position on the issue at hand. Finally, a comprehensive index allows readers to locate content quickly and efficiently.

Introducing Issues with Opposing Viewpoints is also significantly different from Opposing Viewpoints. As the series title implies, its presentation will help introduce students to the concept of opposing viewpoints and learn to use this material to aid in critical writing and debate. The series' four-color, accessible format makes the books attractive and inviting to readers of all levels. In addition, each viewpoint has been carefully edited to maximize a reader's understanding of the content. Short but thorough viewpoints capture the essence of an argument. A substantial, thought-provoking essay question placed at the end of each viewpoint asks the student to further investigate the issues raised in the viewpoint, compare and contrast two authors' arguments, or consider how one might go about forming an opinion on the topic at hand. Each viewpoint contains sidebars that include at-a-glance information and handy statistics. A Facts About section located in the back of the book further supplies students with relevant facts and figures.

Following in the tradition of the Opposing Viewpoints series, Greenhaven Press continues to provide readers with invaluable exposure to the controversial issues that shape our world. As John Stuart Mill once wrote: "The only way in which a human being can make some approach to knowing the whole of a subject is by hearing what can be said about it by persons of every variety of opinion and studying all modes in which it can be looked at by every character of mind. No wise man ever acquired his wisdom in any mode but this." It is to this principle that Introducing Issues with Opposing Viewpoints books are dedicated.

Introduction

"The potential benefits of ocean desalination are great, but the economic, cultural, and environmental costs of wide commercialization remains high."

—Pacific Institute, *Desalination, With a Grain of Salt*, 2006

According to the United Nations Educational, Scientific and Cultural Organization (UNESCO),

> The looming water crisis is one of the most critical challenges facing the world today. Global demand for this precious resource has increased more than sixfold over the past century compared with a threefold increase in world population. Without better management . . . two-thirds of humanity will suffer from severe or moderate shortages by the year 2025.

Because of this impending challenge, water resource managers around the world are increasingly turning to desalination—removing salts from water—to tap into the world's oceans. The leading desalination technologies involve distillation and the use of membranes (filters), both of which mimic Earth's natural water processes. However, both processes are energy intensive, and many desalination technologies require the use of fuels that may contribute to global climate change. While desalination may solve the water problem in the short term, the greenhouse gases it produces may exacerbate the problem in the long term. As a result, scientists are developing new, cleaner technologies for desalination.

In 2004, when Australia was considering a desalination plant, the *Sydney Morning Herald* voiced opposition: "The size of the desalination plant the Government is considering would be able to produce about 100 million litres of water a day and about 255,500 tonnes of greenhouse gas emissions a year." The public found the proposed coal-fired plant to be unacceptable.

In response, planners used a newer technology that creates no greenhouse gases. The Kwinana Desalination Plant—opened in Perth in 2007—has 100 percent of its energy needs met by renewable wind power. Forty-eight huge wind turbines, each as tall as a fifteen-story building, are employed to convert the wind power into electricity.

While this macro technology worked well in Australia, reliable renewable energy sources are not available everywhere. However, a recent breakthrough in nanotechnology could reduce the energy demands of membrane desalination—the most common form of desalination—by 75 percent. Researchers at Lawrence Livermore National Laboratory (LLNL) have created carbon atom nanotubes that are more than fifty thousand times thinner than a human hair. Billions of these nanotubes form a membrane that can quickly separate water molecules from salts. "[The gas and] water flows we measured are one hundred to ten thousand times faster than what classical models predict. This is like having a garden hose that can deliver as much water in the same amount of time as a fire hose that is 10 times larger," said Olgica Bakajin, the lead scientist on the project, in a 2006 press release from the LLNL. This nanotechnology may be the key to desalinating large volumes of ocean water at a low economic cost. This could be a real boon for water resource managers who are scurrying to find a stable water source that is unaffected by rainfall.

The state of California is currently reviewing twenty proposed desalination facilities. If all of these are implemented, the state will have seventy times its current desalination capacity. According to a 2006 report by the Pacific Institute, "Interest in desalination has been especially high in California, where rapidly growing populations, inadequate regulation of water supply/land use nexus, and ecosystem degradation from existing water supply sources have forced a rethinking of water policies and management."

This report raises an unsettling question among many water experts and environmentalists: If the water crisis is largely due to man's mismanagement, then even if new technology were to reduce the desalination energy cost to zero, is desalination really the answer to the water crisis? In other words, does humankind have the right to misuse its supply of naturally occurring freshwater (about 3 percent of Earth's water) and then turn to the ocean as though it were a limitless supply?

A 2007 report on desalination by the World Wide Fund for Nature, also known as the World Wildlife Fund (WWF), reminds people that desalination is "the processing of seawater habitat." In the quest for improved desalination technologies, it is sometimes overlooked that oceans are not just vast bodies of water. Seawater is home to abundant plants and animals.

Rachel Kleinman, reporter for the *Age,* wrote in 2007 about one of the primary fears regarding the impact of desalination: "Most environmental concerns about desalination focus on the effect of the concentrated salt waste, or brine, being pumped back into the ocean. . . . The waste, which is high in iron and salt, is a little-known by-product of the desalination process." This brine is a chief concern of the more than two hundred citizens who met on November 6, 2007, to oppose a desalination plant in their community, Upper Spencer Gulf, Australia. According to ABC (Australian Broadcasting Corporation) News, residents are concerned that "the plant's highly saline discharge would kill the local prawn industry."

In addition to the risk of killing ocean life by its waste output, desalination historically kills ocean creatures by its water intake. "We know that we have lost trillions of fish larvae, but no one's ever quantified their value to the food chain, other than to say that the loss is probably important. We know that they're killed, and at what rate, but beyond that—what is the long term effect to the rest of the ecosystem? We don't have a clue. We've never looked at that," said Pete Raimondi, professor of ecology and evolutionary biology at the University of California at Santa Cruz, in a 2005 interview on desalination with the *Los Angeles Times.*

With ten thousand desalination plants already built around the world, WWF cautions, "The dramatic upscaling of the industry is occurring against a backdrop of unresolved questions on the potential environmental impacts of large scale processing of seawater habitat and the discharge of increasing volumes of concentrate brine."

This discussion of new technology and its impact on desalination and the global water crisis illustrates the importance of examining the various viewpoints on issues that affect life, human and otherwise. Water—one of Earth's simplest and most plentiful resources and yet posing one of the world's most controversial management problems—will be explored from many angles in *Introducing Issues with Opposing Viewpoints: Water Resource Management.* The authors of the viewpoints in this volume explore current water management beliefs, the tools used to manage water resources, and potential solutions to water resource problems.

Chapter 1

What Current Beliefs Guide Water Management?

World Water Day, designated by the United Nations to promote conservation and development of water resources, occurs every March 22nd.

Global Warming Creates a Water Crisis

"If global warming has shifted climate conditions closer to those that existed prior to 5,200 years ago, high-altitude glaciers may be under wholesale retreat and may disappear altogether 'in the near future . . .'"

Peter N. Spotts

In the following viewpoint Peter N. Spotts cites data from United Nations reports asserting that greenhouse gas emissions have led to global warming, which has contributed to drought conditions, and that such conditions are likely to worsen over time. Spotts describes water conservation efforts employed by the city of Albuquerque, New Mexico, and planning underway by other cities around the world. Peter N. Spotts is a staff writer for *The Christian Science Monitor.*

AS YOU READ, CONSIDER THE FOLLOWING QUESTIONS:
1. According to James McCarthy, cited in this viewpoint, what happens when you have a pattern of droughts alternating with strong downpours?

2. What steps has the city of Albuquerque, New Mexico, taken to reduce water consumption?
3. How is Quito, Ecuador, planning to deal with the retreat of the Antizana glacier that is their current primary source of water?

I t's a late March morning, and a light breeze tousles the tops of aspens and Ponderosa pines at Elk Cabin, one of the oldest spots in New Mexico for recording the depth of winter snow. Richard Armijo, a measuring stick in hand, is there to gauge this spring's snowpack.

The site, in the Sangre de Cristo Mountains, sits just upstream from two reservoirs that serve the city of Santa Fe. In late March, Elk Cabin should have a foot of snow on the ground, but it's nearly bare.

Like much of the West, New Mexico has endured a long drought.

According to the latest scientific evidence, such dry spells are likely to grow more severe—as they will around the world. Global warming, climate scientists say, is changing climates from the Himalayan Mountains to the Euphrates-Tigris River Basin. Patterns of rain and snowfall are shifting significantly.

Water Shortage Ahead

The question now becomes: How will nations and individuals adapt as Earth's climate warms? Glaciers from the Andes to the Alps are shrinking at an accelerating pace. Countries are already haggling over river rights. From 400 million to as many as 3.2 billion people face serious water shortages over the next 20 to 50 years. New Mexico, an already dry region that is getting drier, is on the front lines.

Mr. Armijo, a snow surveyor for the US Department of Agriculture, knows something is going on. Like much of the American West, the state has been in the grip of drought for years.

"We've set record lows for snowpack a couple of times in the last five or six years," he says. "For the most part, the snowpack's gone. In the last three to four weeks, we've experienced some really warm temperatures."

In early February, the UN released a report on the science behind global warming. In it, researchers expressed "very high confidence" that greenhouse-gas emissions—mostly carbon dioxide from burning coal, oil, and natural gas—have been warming the climate.

Wrong Form, Wrong Time

If these emissions continue to grow at their current rates, the report estimates, global average temperatures could top their 1980–2000 average by 2.3 to 4.1 degrees C. (4.1 to 7.4 degrees F.) by the end of the century. Among the warming's effects: Arid regions will dry out further. And some of the water that they do receive will come in the wrong form (rain instead of snow) or at the wrong time.

On April 6 the UN-sponsored Intergovernmental Panel on Climate Change (IPCC) will release the second of its four major global-warming reports due this year. The focus: the challenges that vulnerable regions are likely to face and their options for adapting.

The new IPCC report is expected to pay close attention to warming's impact on water resources—and for good reason, says James McCarthy, professor of biological oceanography at Harvard University

Changes in Global Average Temperatures, 1850–2000

Taken from: Intergovernmental Panel on Climate Change, 2007.

and past co-chairman of the 2001 IPCC working group. In the last five years, scientists have seen "a consistent record" showing a pattern of droughts alternating with strong downpours "with less opportunity for that moisture to be absorbed or retained," Dr. McCarthy says.

A City Slakes Its Thirst

How will humans cope with a drier climate? The city of Albuquerque has shown how much water can be saved through a concerted effort—if resources are available. But its experience also highlights the complex demands made on water resources.

The state's major river, the Rio Grande, cuts through Albuquerque. But it's only a dry riverbed part of the year. The city draws virtually all of its water from an underground aquifer, says John Stomp III, water resources manager for the city. By some accounts, Albuquerque once was thought to be sitting atop an aquifer with enough fresh water to fill Lake Michigan.

But in 1993, a closer look reversed that verdict: The city's underground lake was far smaller than previously estimated—and it was disappearing fast.

In 1994, the city set a goal to cut water consumption by 30 percent over 10 years. By 2004, it had cut consumption by 33 percent. By 2014, it aims to reduce that to 40 percent below 1994 levels.

To meet its goals, the city tightened its building code to improve efficient use of water. It gave tax rebates to residents and businesses for each low-flow toilet or shower head installed in existing buildings. It offered a $100 credit for installing water-efficient washing machines. It gave rebates for xeriscaping—replacing water-hungry lawns and plants with drought-tolerant species—and it changed landscaping codes to require this approach in new developments. The city also irrigates its parks and other public lands with treated municipal wastewater and has been hunting down and repairing leaky water mains.

Sending Water Back Underground

Albuquerque also has built a diversion dam across the Rio Grande and is completing an enormous water-distribution facility nearby. Both open for business next year.

When they do, the city will rely on river water for 70 percent of its needs and use the underground aquifer to make up for shortfalls during dry years. During wet years, it plans to use some of the Rio Grande water to recharge the aquifer.

While the new IPCC reports may begin to add new urgency to water planning, up until now it's been difficult to factor global warming into water-resource plans, Mr. Stomp says.

The earlier models he's relied upon have given conflicting answers to questions surrounding local precipitation.

"One says there's going to be more snow; one says there's going to be less snow," he says. But planning for severe, prolonged droughts has always been part of the planning process, he says.

Wastewater-to-Drinking-Water Conversion

Over the long term, population growth is likely to push other water-saving approaches to the fore, such as desalination of brackish underground water and reuse of municipal wastewater for drinking. At least six cities in the state are considering wastewater-to-drinking-water conversions either through a direct treatment and recycling system or by using treated wastewater to recharge aquifers.

Ironically, such efforts could make it more difficult for the state to balance the competing demands of its urban and rural interests. It will also be harder to meet its obligations to send some of its river water on to Texas, says John D'Antonio, New Mexico's state engineer.

In the West, agriculture consumes most of the water. Many farmers here are installing more-efficient irrigation systems that lose less water to seepage as it moves along irrigation ditches. But that "leaking" water also contributes to groundwater reserves. Now less water is finding its way back into aquifers.

Water is a finite resource, Mr. D'Antonio notes. If rivers are fully subscribed, the only way for the state to grow is to transfer water rights in an orderly way from agriculture to urban uses.

FAST FACT

Former vice president Al Gore inspired and starred in a 2006 documentary film about global warming—*An Inconvenient Truth*—and was awarded an Oscar and the Nobel Peace Prize.

A Thirsty World Responds to Scarcity

How issues like these will play out around the world will depend on many factors, including whether countries can work out disputes over water resources.

So far, the record is patchy. In the Philippines, researchers from Columbia University are trying to help the city of Manila set up a water-leasing deal with nearby farmers. The city and farmers share a small reservoir—and recurring drought.

But in dry years, the city typically has just taken all the water it needed, leading to "massive agricultural losses," says Casey Brown, a member of the group working on the water-lease project. The hope is to set up a plan under which the city would pay the farmers for the water it takes during droughts—providing, among other things, an added economic incentive for the city to conserve during dry years.

Political instability can get in the way, too.

Several years of drought have caused water levels to drop, leaving a "bathtub ring" around the edge of Lake Mead north of Hoover Dam.

Iraq, Syria, and Turkey have formed a joint commission on water issues, but it hasn't met since the first Gulf War in 1992, says Olcay Unver, a visiting scholar at the Water Resources Research Institute at Kent State University in Kent, Ohio.

Ironically, global warming may provide a catalyst by forcing countries to work together to solve their mutual problem, he suggests. "All parties see it as a common threat—which it is," Mr. Unver says. "So it could provide the basis for common solutions to water management."

High Glaciers Retreating Fast

Hundreds of millions of people around the world draw their water from major river systems whose sources are mountain glaciers and seasonal snowpack. From the Andes and Himalayas to the Alps, scientists are gathering data that tell a sobering tale of rapidly retreating tongues of ice.

The World Glacier Monitoring Service tracks 27 glaciers in nine mountain ranges around the world. The service's data show that these glaciers have been steadily losing mass since 1980.

This comes as no surprise to Lonnie Thompson. Since 1983 he has studied ice cores from mountain glaciers and ice caps in the Andes, Himalayas, and from Mt. Kilimanjaro in Tanzania. Last July, the Ohio State University professor and his colleagues published a paper suggesting that the current warming at high elevations is unprecedented in the last 2,000 years; in some areas, warming and the pace of glacial retreat is unprecedented for the past 5,200 years.

For example, the Qori Kalis glacier, the largest outlet for the Quelccaya ice cap in Peru, retreated 10 times faster during the 1990s than it did from 1963 to 1978, Dr. Thompson says. "The changes are overwhelming."

If global warming has shifted climate conditions closer to those that existed prior to 5,200 years ago, high-altitude glaciers may be under wholesale retreat and may disappear altogether "in the near future," Thompson says.

Already, some cities relying on these natural water towers are struggling to adapt. But these efforts are at their early stages, according to Walter Vergara, a civil engineer with the World Bank. In Quito, Ecuador, for example, the city of 2 million relies on water from the fast-retreating Antizana glacier. Quito has laid out pipeline and reservoir projects to expand its water supplies to keep pace with the city's growth through 2040. But the plans haven't factored in global warming, Mr. Vergara says.

Quito is now trying to anticipate the glacier's retreat and changing patterns of precipitation. This means extending water pipelines farther up the mountain and around the back of the glacier to tap its eastern, Amazon Basin side. The changes will add $100 million to the $300 million project, Vergara estimates.

Managing water supplies in a warmer, more variable climate "is a challenge developing countries face right now," notes Casey Brown, a climate scientist at Columbia University. "If they can meet this challenge, they'll be in much better shape to meet [the] other challenges [that] climate change brings."

EVALUATING THE AUTHOR'S ARGUMENTS:

The author of this viewpoint presents water conservation methods being used in urban and rural settings as well as the role governments can play in encouraging conservation. Citing examples from the viewpoint, what methods seem like they will prove most successful?

Global Warming Is Exaggerated

Freeman J. Dyson

"I am not saying that the warming does not cause problems. . . . I am saying that the problems are grossly exaggerated."

Scientist Freeman J. Dyson is a self-proclaimed heretic—a disputer of scientific dogma. In the following viewpoint, taken from his recently published book, *Many-Colored Glass: Reflections on the Place of Life in the Universe,* Dyson takes issue with the widely held belief that global warming is global and that it is a crisis. Instead of accepting global warming as a model for the future, Dyson presents alternative scientific scenarios. He also reminds people that real science is more dependent on real observation of real life by real people and less dependent on computer-generated models. Dyson, a professor of physics at the Institute for Advanced Study in Princeton, is known for his work in quantum mechanics and nuclear weapons design.

AS YOU READ, CONSIDER THE FOLLOWING QUESTIONS:

1. The author asks readers to remember the number "one-hundredth of an inch per year." How does he explain what that number means?
2. When the author listens to the public debates about climate change, what impresses him?
3. According to this viewpoint, what is the most alarming possible cause of sea-level rise?

Freeman J. Dyson, *A Many-Colored Glass: Reflections on the Place of Life in the Universe,* Charlottesville: University of Virginia Press, 2007. Copyright © 2007 by the Rector and Visitors of the University of Virginia. All rights reserved. Reproduced with permission of the University of Virginia Press.

My first heresy [departure from an accepted theory] says that all the fuss about global warming is grossly exaggerated. Here I am opposing the holy brotherhood of climate model experts and the crowd of deluded citizens who believe the numbers predicted by the computer models. Of course, they say, I have no degree in meteorology and I am therefore not qualified to speak. But I have studied the climate models and I know what they can do. The models solve the equations of fluid dynamics, and they do a very good job of describing the fluid motions of the atmosphere and the oceans. They do a very poor job of describing the clouds, the dust, the chemistry, and the biology of fields and farms and forests. They do not begin to describe the real world that we live in. The real world is muddy and messy and full of things that we do not yet understand. It is much easier for a scientist to sit in an air-conditioned building and run computer models than to put on winter clothes and measure what is really happening outside in the swamps and the clouds. That is why the climate model experts end up believing their own models.

There is no doubt that parts of the world are getting warmer, but the warming is not global. I am not saying that the warming does not cause problems. Obviously it does. Obviously we should be trying to understand it better. I am saying that the problems are grossly exaggerated. They take away money and attention from other problems that are more urgent and more important, such as poverty and infectious disease and public education and public health, and the preservation of living creatures on land and in the oceans, not to mention easy problems such as the timely construction of adequate dikes around the city of New Orleans.

Tracking Carbon Dioxide Is Important

I will discuss the global warming problem in detail because it is interesting, even though its importance is exaggerated. One of the main causes of warming is the increase of carbon dioxide in the atmosphere resulting from our burning of fossil fuels such as oil and coal and natural gas. To understand the movement of carbon through the atmosphere and biosphere, we need to measure a lot of numbers. I do not want to confuse you with a lot of numbers, so I will ask you to remember just one number. The number that I ask

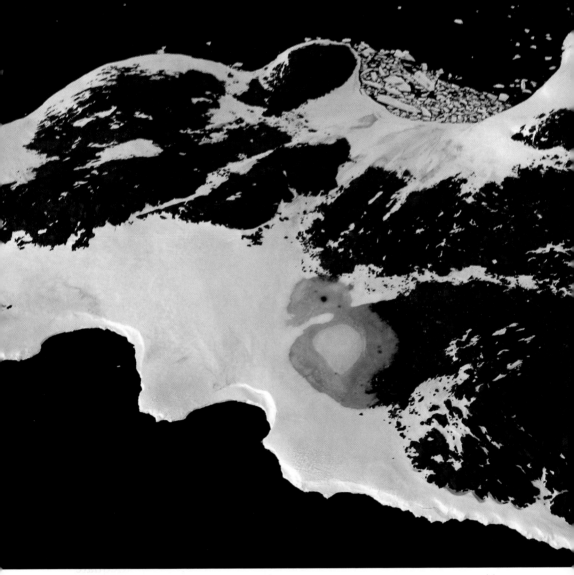

Melting snow forms a lake near Cape Folger, Antarctica.

you to remember is one-hundredth of an inch per year. Now I will explain what this number means. Consider the half of the land area of the earth that is not desert or ice cap or city or road or parking lot. This is the half of the land that is covered with soil and supports vegetation of one kind or another. Every year it absorbs and converts into biomass a certain fraction of the carbon dioxide that we emit into the atmosphere. Biomass means living creatures, plants and microbes and animals, and the organic materials that are left behind when the creatures die and decay. We don't know how big a fraction of our emissions is absorbed by the land, since we have not measured the increase or decrease of the biomass. The number that I ask you to remember is the increase in thickness, averaged over one-half of the land area of the planet, of the biomass that would result if all the carbon that we are emitting by burning fossil fuels were absorbed. The average increase in thickness is one-hundredth of an inch per year.

The point of this calculation is the very favorable rate of exchange between carbon in the atmosphere and carbon in the soil. To stop the carbon in the atmosphere from increasing, we only need to grow the biomass in the soil by a hundredth of an inch per year. Good topsoil contains about 10 percent biomass so a hundredth of an inch of biomass growth means about a tenth of an inch of topsoil. Changes in farming practices such as no-till farming, avoiding the use of the plow, cause biomass to grow at least as fast as this. If we plant crops without plowing the soil, more of the biomass goes into roots that stay in the soil, and less returns to the atmosphere. If we use genetic engineering to put more biomass into roots, we can probably achieve much more rapid growth of topsoil. I conclude from this calculation that the problem of carbon dioxide in the atmosphere is a problem of land management, not a problem of meteorology. No computer model of atmosphere and ocean can hope to predict the way we shall manage our land. . . .

The Warming Is Local, Not Global

When I listen to the public debates about climate change, I am impressed by the enormous gaps in our knowledge, the sparseness of our observations, and the superficiality of our theories. Many of the basic processes of planetary ecology are poorly understood. They must be better understood before we can reach an accurate diagnosis of the present condition of our planet. When we are trying to take care of a planet, just as when we are taking care of a human patient, diseases must be diagnosed before they can be cured. We need to

A Simplified Look at Global Warming and the "Greenhouse Effect"

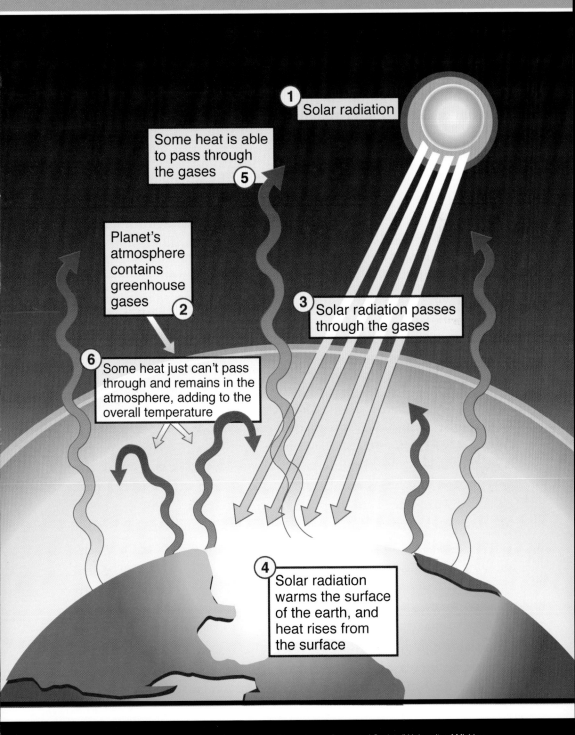

1 Solar radiation

Some heat is able to pass through the gases 5

Planet's atmosphere contains greenhouse gases 2

3 Solar radiation passes through the gases

6 Some heat just can't pass through and remains in the atmosphere, adding to the overall temperature

4 Solar radiation warms the surface of the earth, and heat rises from the surface

observe and measure what is going on in the biosphere, rather than rely on computer models.

Everyone agrees that the increasing abundance of carbon dioxide in the atmosphere has two important consequences, first a change in the physics of radiation transport in the atmosphere, and second a change in the biology of plants on the ground and in the ocean. Opinions differ on the relative importance of the physical and biological effects, and on whether the effects, either separately or together, are beneficial or harmful. The physical effects are seen in changes of rainfall, cloudiness, wind strength, and temperature, which are customarily lumped together in the misleading phrase *global warming*. In humid air, the effect of carbon dioxide on radiation transport is unimportant because the transport of thermal radiation is already blocked by the much larger greenhouse effect of water vapor. The effect of carbon dioxide is important where the air is dry, and air is usually dry only where it is cold. Hot desert air may feel dry but often contains a lot of water vapor. The warming effect of carbon dioxide is strongest where air is cold and dry, mainly in the Arctic rather than in the tropics, mainly in mountainous regions rather than in lowlands, mainly in winter rather than in summer, and mainly at night rather than in daytime. The warming is real, but it is mostly making cold places warmer rather than making hot places hotter. To represent this local warming by a global average is misleading. . . .

West Antarctic Ice Sheet

The most alarming possible cause of sea-level rise is a rapid disintegration of the West Antarctic ice sheet, which is the part of Antarctica where the bottom of the ice is far below sea level. Warming seas around the edge of Antarctica might erode the ice cap from below and cause it to collapse into the ocean. If the whole of West Antarctica disintegrated rapidly, sea level would rise by five meters, with disastrous effects on billions of people. However, recent measurements of the ice cap show that it is not losing volume fast enough to make a significant contribution to the currently observed sea-level rise. It appears that the warming seas around Antarctica are causing an increase in snowfall over the ice cap, and the increased snowfall on top roughly cancels out the decrease of ice volume caused by erosion at the edges. The same changes, increased melting of ice at the edges and increased snowfall adding ice on top, are also observed in Greenland. In addition, there is an increase in snowfall over the East Antarctic ice cap, which is much larger and colder and is in no danger of melting. This is another situation where we do not know how much of the environmental change is due to human activities and how much to long-term natural processes over which we have no control.

Global Warming Has Caused Water Scarcity

Donald Wilhite, David Diodato, et al.

"In late July 2006, drought affected more than 50% of the United States."

According to the following 2007 report by the Geological Society of America, risk of drought, or natural water scarcity, is increasing. Particularly since the mid-1990s, droughts have been increasing in spatial extent (percentage of the contiguous United States affected), severity (number of consecutive years of drought), and impact (economic, environmental, and social). The authors assert that global climate change is a significant factor contributing to drought. Higher temperatures result in accelerated evaporation from bodies of water and an increased need for water by vegetation, according to the authors. The Geological Society of America, founded in 1888, promotes the geosciences and fosters the professional growth of earth scientists.

AS YOU READ, CONSIDER THE FOLLOWING QUESTIONS:

1. According to this viewpoint, what do recent severe droughts in the United States, beginning in 1996, indicate?

Donald Wilhite et al., *Managing Drought: A Roadmap for Change in the United States*, Boulder, CO: The Geological Society of America. A report from Managing Drought and Water Scarcity in Vulnerable Environments, 2007. Reproduced by permission. www.geosociety.org/meetings/06drought/roadmap.pdf.

2. What do the authors state is the expected change in annual average precipitation?
3. According to the authors, what are the most important droughts in any region?

Drought hazard is the likelihood that an area will be affected by drought in the future. Virtually all parts of the United States are drought-prone, and drought occurs somewhere in the country each year. Since 1895, approximately 15% of the United States has been affected by drought in any given year. Droughts of the 1930s, 1950s, and 1999 to present [July 2007] were particularly severe and long, affecting vast areas. At its peak spatial extent in 1934, 65% of the contiguous United States was affected by severe to extreme drought conditions.

Drought Hazard Is Growing

Recent severe droughts in the United States—beginning in 1996 and affecting nearly all parts of the country—are indicative of the growing drought hazard. For many regions, drought has occurred for five or more consecutive years. Montana and surrounding states and portions of the Great Plains experienced severe drought for seven or more consecutive drought years. Arizona and New Mexico experienced five consecutive years of drought during this same period. In 2006, drought was particularly severe in the Great Plains region, extending from Texas and Oklahoma in the south to the Dakotas in the north. Parts of Nebraska have also experienced seven consecutive years of drought. At its peak spatial extent and severity in late July 2006, drought affected more than 50% of the United States. Drought is not just a southwestern issue. For example, Florida, Georgia, North Carolina, and South Carolina all experienced three to four consecutive years of drought between 1999 and 2002. Drought conditions have recurred in that region in 2007, affecting most of Alabama, Florida, Georgia, Mississippi, and Tennessee. Severe drought has also struck Minnesota and Wisconsin, areas many regard as water-rich.

This map shows drought in the conterminous United States, June 26, 2007.

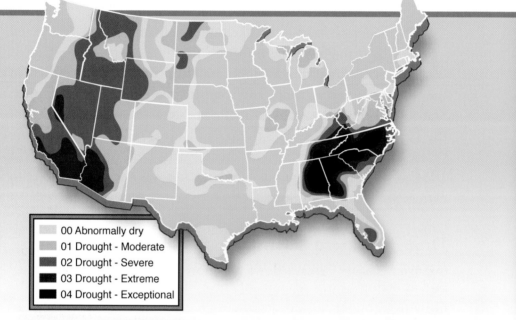

00 Abnormally dry
01 Drought - Moderate
02 Drought - Severe
03 Drought - Extreme
04 Drought - Exceptional

Taken from: National Drought Mitigation Center.

Global Climate Change Affects Drought Hazard

Global climate change is now recognized as a major new factor that must be considered in assessing future drought hazard. Climate has changed many times over Earth's history, and climate will continue to change in the future. The current pace of global climate change, which is unprecedented in recorded human history, is likely to significantly influence future drought hazard. Because of the magnitude of global climate change, historical data may not be as useful an indicator in estimating future drought hazard as it has been traditionally viewed. Despite the complexity of the coupled and interacting phenomena, there exists broad scientific consensus that global climate change will affect temperature, precipitation, evaporation, transpiration of water by plants, surface-water flow, and ground-water recharge. In particular, there is high confidence that global climate change will lead to higher average temperatures nearly everywhere.

Higher temperatures tend to increase evaporation and vegetative demand for water (transpiration) and consequently are likely to reduce water available for stream flow and ground-water recharge. Estimates for the Colorado River Basin that consider the influence of temperature range from small to quite significant reductions of flow. Increased evaporation results in greater losses from surface-water bodies and reservoirs.

Snow Slows Water Flow

In the United States, annual average precipitation is expected to change less than 10%, with slight increases on the northern border and slight decreases on the southern border. Local regions such as the Sierra Nevada and Rocky Mountains, however, may see more (and warmer) precipitation in winter and less in spring and early summer. When the character of precipitation changes from slowly melting winter snowpacks or regular seasonal rains to short-duration, high-intensity storms, stream flows are more erratic, less ground-water recharge occurs, and the reliability of ground-water and surface-water reservoirs declines.

Drought Is Difficult to Predict

At present, scientists have limited ability to predict drought. Lead times of interest range from a week or two to a season or two for "operational" purposes. Drought

> **FAST FACT**
>
> Every year World Water Day is celebrated on March 22. In 2007 the theme was Coping with Water Scarcity.

likelihood on multi-year and decadal scales represents a different type of prediction. Water managers and operators of large reservoir systems are interested in multi-year and decadal predictions because they have sufficient storage capacity to allow them to make operational adjustments over that time period.

The most important droughts in any region are usually those that affect the main precipitation season(s). Causes vary: winter snowpack,

A boat is stranded along Lake Okeechobee in Florida as water levels drop exposing grass and dried silt.

summer convection, the Southwest monsoon, tropical storms, cool season cyclones, "the pineapple express" on the West Coast, spring instability showers, frontal passages, sea breezes, nor'easters, lake effect snow, and others. In regions where multiple causes produce multiple precipitation seasons, lengthy droughts are less likely.

EVALUATING THE AUTHORS' ARGUMENTS:

According to this viewpoint, "Virtually all parts of the United States are drought-prone, and drought occurs somewhere in the country each year." Based on that statement, in your opinion, what responsibility, if any, do states have when a neighboring state is experiencing a severe drought?

Viewpoint

4

Social and Political Factors Have Led to Water Scarcity

Kevin Watkins

"The scarcity at the heart of the global water crisis is rooted in power, poverty and inequality, not in physical availability."

The following viewpoint, taken from a 2006 report by the United Nations Development Programme (UNDP), states that more than 1 billion people in developing countries lack access to clean water, and 2.6 billion people live without basic sanitation. According to the authors, the water problem in such nations is due not to scarcity or a physical lack of water but to political and institutional policies that deny the poor access to clean water. While other global health crises, such as the spread of HIV/AIDS and the threat of the avian flu pandemic, have sparked worldwide action, the water crisis has been largely ignored because, the authors assert, it is a problem that primarily affects the poor. The UNDP is the United Nations' global development network, helping developing countries find solutions to problems like poverty and disease. Kevin Watkins is the director of the UNDP Human Development Report Office.

AS YOU READ, CONSIDER THE FOLLOWING QUESTIONS:
1. According to this viewpoint, in high-income areas of cities in Asia, Latin America, and sub-Saharan Africa, what kind of water privileges do people enjoy?
2. What factors combine to deny poor people access to water, in the author's view?
3. How does the author of this viewpoint define "water security"?

Some commentators trace the global challenge in water to a problem of scarcity. The spirit of Thomas Malthus, who in the 19th century disconcerted political leaders by predicting a future of food shortages, increasingly pervades international debates on water. With population rising and demands on the world's water expanding, so the argument runs, the future points to a "gloomy arithmetic" of shortage. We reject this starting point. The availability of water is a concern for some countries. But the scarcity at the heart of the global water crisis is rooted in power, poverty and inequality, not in physical availability.

The Wealthy Have Better Access

Nowhere is this more apparent than in the area of water for life. Today, some 1.1 billion people in developing countries have inadequate access to water, and 2.6 billion lack basic sanitation. Those twin deficits are rooted in institutions and political choices, not in water's availability. Household water requirements represent a tiny fraction of water use, usually less than 5% of the total, but there is tremendous inequality in access to clean water, and to sanitation at a household level. In high-income areas of cities in Asia, Latin America and Sub-Saharan Africa people enjoy access to several hundred litres of water a day delivered into their homes at low prices by public utilities. Meanwhile, slum dwellers and poor households in rural areas of the same countries have access to much less than the 20 litres of water a day per person required to meet the most basic human needs. Women and young girls carry a double burden of disadvantage, since they are the ones who sacrifice their time and their education to collect water.

Homeless children in Zimbabwe collect drinking water from a water main located under the street.

Much the same applies to water for livelihoods. Across the world agriculture and industry are adjusting to tightening hydrological constraints. But while scarcity is a widespread problem, it is not experienced by all. In water-stressed parts of India irrigation pumps extract water from aquifers 24 hours a day for wealthy farmers, while neighbouring smallholders depend on the vagaries of rain. Here, too, the underlying cause of scarcity in the large majority of cases is institutional and political, not a physical deficiency of supplies. In many countries scarcity is the product of public policies that have encouraged overuse of water through subsidies and underpricing.

Poor People Are Excluded

There is more than enough water in the world for domestic purposes, for agriculture and for industry. The problem is that some people—notably the poor—are systematically excluded from access by their poverty, by their limited legal rights or by public policies that limit access to the infrastructures that provide water for life and for livelihoods. In short, scarcity is manufactured through political processes and institutions that disadvantage the poor. When it comes to clean water, the pattern in many countries is that the poor get less, pay more and bear the brunt of the human development costs associated with scarcity.

Water Security Creates Human Security

Just over a decade ago *Human Development Report 1994* introduced the idea of human security to the wider debate on development. The aim was to look beyond narrow perceptions of national security, defined in terms of military threats and the protection of strategic foreign policy goals, and towards a vision of security rooted in the lives of people.

Water security is an integral part of this broader conception of human security. In broad terms water security is about ensuring that every person has reliable access to enough safe water at an affordable price to lead a healthy,

FAST FACT

The amount of water on Earth has not changed since Earth was formed; it is consumption of water that has changed. Globally, consumption has increased nearly tenfold since 1900.

dignified and productive life, while maintaining the ecological systems that provide water and also depend on water. When these conditions are not met, or when access to water is disrupted, people face acute human security risks transmitted through poor health and the disruption of livelihoods.

Unclean Water Kills More People than Wars Do

In the world of the early 21st century national security concerns loom large on the international agenda. Violent conflict, concerns over terrorist threats, the proliferation of nuclear weapons and the growth of illicit trade in arms and drugs all pose acute challenges. Against this backdrop it is easy to lose sight of some basic human security imperatives including those linked to water. The 1.8 million child deaths each year related to unclean water and poor sanitation dwarf the casualties associated with violent conflict. No act of terrorism generates economic devastation on the scale of the crisis in water and sanitation. Yet the issue barely registers on the international agenda.

It is not just the contrast with national security imperatives that is striking. Today, international action to tackle the crisis in HIV/AIDS has been institutionalized on the agenda of the Group of Eight countries. Threatened with a potential public health crisis in the form of avian flu, the world mobilizes rapidly to draw up a global plan of

Clean Water Is a Basic Human Right

The United Nations wants all people to have access to at least 5.28 gallons of clean water per person per day. Amercians use an average of 100 gallons of clean water per person per day.

Gallons of Water

100	
50	
5	
0	

| 5.28 Gallons | 100 gallons |

Compiled by editor

action. But the living reality of the water and sanitation crisis elicits only the most minimal and fragmented response. Why is that? One plausible explanation is that, unlike HIV/AIDS and avian flu, the water and sanitation crisis poses the most immediate and most direct threat to poor people in poor countries—a constituency that lacks a voice in shaping national and international perceptions of human security.

EVALUATING THE AUTHORS' ARGUMENTS:

The previous viewpoint describes an increasingly severe drought hazard, particularly in the American West, due to global warming. In this viewpoint the global community is urged to take responsibility to provide clean water to people in all nations. In your opinion, how should wealthy nations balance the need to solve their own water problems with the need to help people in developing nations? Give reasons for your answer.

Water Is Best Managed by Privatization

Ronald Bailey

"Imperfect privatization efforts have already successfully connected millions of poor people to relatively inexpensive water where government-funded efforts have failed."

According to award-winning science journalist Ronald Bailey, activists say "water is a human right" and therefore should be protected and guaranteed for every person by the global community or local governments. However, the global community is failing to raise the needed funds to help even half the people without access to safe drinking water. Historically, local governments in developing countries have found the money to provide water and even subsidies for their minority of wealthy citizens, while leaving the majority of citizens—poor people—without access to piped clean water. The author suggests that while privatization (allowing private companies to sell, distribute, and manage water for a profit) is not a perfect solution, it is a solution that allows disadvantaged people to have access to piped clean water. Ronald Bailey is science correspondent for the monthly magazine *Reason*, which is published by the Reason Foundation, a libertarian think tank.

1. According to this viewpoint, what case does Fredrik Segerfeldt make for privatization in his book *Water for Sale*?
2. In Ronald Bailey's view, what does Segerfeldt show about water privatization in Guinea?
3. What does Bailey describe as the "activist myth" concerning privatization efforts in Cochabamba, Bolivia, and what does he say really happened?

Activists around the world chant the slogan that "water is a human right." Yet more than a billion poor people in the world today lack access to safe drinking water. Twelve million of them die each year from drinking disease-contaminated water.

Among things that would most benefit the world, safe, clean drinking water is clearly a high priority, as pointed out by the Copenhagen Consensus organized by skeptical environmentalist Bjorn Lomborg in 2004.

In 2003 the U.N.'s *World Water Development Report* estimated an annual shortfall of $110 billion to $180 billion in investments needed to provide access to safe water to the poor in the developing world. The U.N.'s Millennium Development Project has a target of reducing by half the proportion of people without access to safe drinking water by 2015. The economic benefits of halving the number of people without access to safe water—in terms of disease avoided, lives lengthened, and time wasted fetching it—add up to $300 billion to $400 billion annually.

Some Governments Fail to Provide Water

Displaying a surprising lack of imagination, the summary of the Copenhagen Consensus paper on water adopted the conventional wisdom that "water service provision has generally been seen as a government responsibility. This is largely because water is regarded as a public good and its availability as a basic human right, best administered by the public sector." Given the fact that so many of the governments in developing countries have somehow failed to recognize their citizens' supposed right to water, perhaps there is a better way to go?

In his excellent new monograph, *Water for Sale: How Business and the Market Can Resolve the World's Water Crisis*, Swedish analyst Fredrik Segerfeldt makes the case that water privatization can go a long way toward quenching the thirst of the poor. Segerfeldt points out that public water systems in developing countries generally supply politically connected wealthy and middle class people, whereas the poor are not hooked up to municipal water mains. Segerfeldt cites one study of 15 countries that found that in the poorest quarters of their populations, 80 percent of the people were not hooked up to water mains. Of course, the poor don't just die of thirst; they just pay more—generally a lot more—for their water.

"Contractors often drive tankers to poor districts, selling water by the can, in which case the very poorest of the world's inhabit-

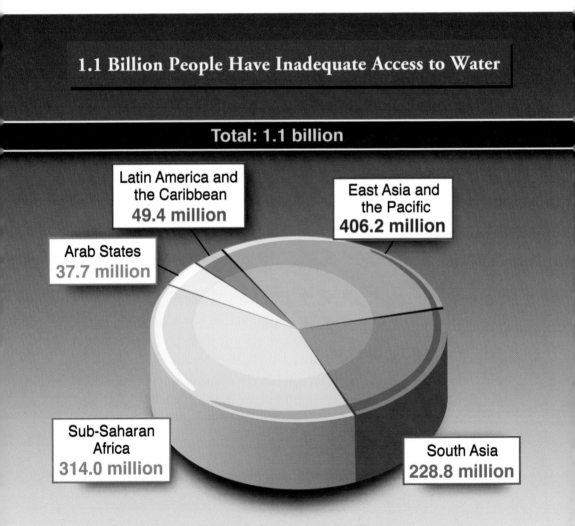

1.1 Billion People Have Inadequate Access to Water

Total: 1.1 billion

Latin America and the Caribbean
49.4 million

East Asia and the Pacific
406.2 million

Arab States
37.7 million

Sub-Saharan Africa
314.0 million

South Asia
228.8 million

Taken from: United Nations Development Programme (UNDP), *Human Development Report*, 2006.

ants are already exposed to market forces but on very unfair terms, because water obtained like this is on average twelve times more expensive than water from regular water mains, and often still more expensive than that," notes Segerfeldt. A survey of major cities in developing countries found that the poor in Lagos, Nigeria pay four to 10 times more for their water than people who are hooked up to water mains do; in Karachi, Pakistan they pay 28 to 83 times more; in Jakarta, Indonesia, four to 60 times; and in Lima, Peru, 17 times more. Essentially, the rich get cheap tap water while the poor pay the moral equivalent of Perrier prices.

Privatization Can Help

So now some countries have turned to the private sector and multi-national companies for help in providing their thirsty poor citizens with water. Privatization can mean selling entire water supply and treatment systems to private owners; long-term leases of water supply systems; or contracts to manage public water systems. In practical terms, the usual arrangement is a long-term lease. So far, only 3 percent of the poor in developing countries get their water from private-sector water systems. However, these initial projects have provoked an outcry by anti-privatization activists around the world against a "global water grab" by giant corporations.

Segerfeldt shows that even imperfect privatization efforts have already successfully connected millions of poor people to relatively inexpensive water where government-funded efforts have failed. For example, before privatization in 1989, only 20 percent of urban dwellers in the African nation of Guinea had access to safe drinking water; by 2001 70 percent did. The price of piped water increased from 15 cents per cubic meter to almost $1, but as Segerfeldt correctly notes, "before privatization the majority of Guineans had no access to mains water at all. They do now. And for these people, the cost of water has fallen drastically. The moral issue, then, is whether it was worth raising the price for the minority of people already connected before privatization in order to reach the 70 percent connected today." In Cartagena, Colombia privatization boosted the number of people receiving piped water by 27 percent. Even the conflicted privatization in Buenos Aires saw the number of households connected to piped water rise by 3 million and 85 percent of the new customers lived in the poor suburbs of the city. Segerfeldt cites other successful privatizations in Gabon, Cambodia, Indonesia, and Morocco.

Privatization Is Not a Perfect Solution

But given the often corrupt governments with which corporations must deal, it's not surprising that privatization can be done very badly. Probably the most spectacular case of privatization gone wrong occurred in Cochabamba, Bolivia. Cochabamba is to anti-privatization activists what the Alamo is to Texans. Between 1989 and 1999, the proportion of households connected to the public water system fell from 70 percent to 60 percent. Water was only sporadically available. In the wealthier neighborhoods 99 percent of households were receiving the subsidized water, while in some poorer suburbs less than 4 percent were connected.

The activist myth is that the poor rose up when the evil multinational Bechtel raised the price of water by 43 percent to 60 percent, depending on the customer's income. While it is true that the lucky few of the poorest who were connected to municipal water supplies did see big increases in their water bills, the majority of the poor who stood to be connected for the first time would have paid much less than they were already paying to water vendors. Segerfeldt calculates that piped water prices were already so low that this would mean the poorest 5 percent of the population would be spending 5.4 percent of their incomes on water. Segerfeldt reports that the opposition to privatization was actually led by middle class and industrial users who had been receiving subsidized water. Opponents also included local water vendors and small farmers who wrongly believed that they were forbidden to access well water.

Without Privatization the Poor Bear an Unfair Burden

Under pressure, Bechtel pulled out and Cochabamba's water supply system is once again being run by the old public utility. Segerfeldt

More than 2,000 protestors demonstrate against a 20 percent increase in the rates charged by the privately owned water processing and distribution plant in Cochabamba, Bolivia.

claims that water is now available only four hours per day and that no new households at all have been connected to the network since 2000. Meanwhile, the poor are paying 10 times more for their water than are the rich households connected to the system. This is a victory for the poor?

Privatization is not a panacea, but Segerfeldt shows that, when properly done, it can play a huge role in bringing safe clean drinking water to the hundreds of millions of people who still lack it. In the meantime, Segerfeldt wonders, "why anti-privatization activists do not expend as much energy on accusing governments of violating the rights of 1.1 billion people who do not have access to water as they do on trying to stop its commercialization." Good question.

EVALUATING THE AUTHOR'S ARGUMENTS:

In this viewpoint Ronald Bailey argues that even though the poor citizens of Cochabamba, Bolivia, dealt with water price increases of 43 to 60 percent under privatization by the corporation Bechtel, they were better off than before because they had been paying even more to local water vendors. Do you think his argument justifies Bechtel's price increases? Why or why not?

Viewpoint

6

Clean Water Should Be Guaranteed by Government

"Uruguay ... became the first nation in the world to introduce a constitutional amendment declaring water resources a public good and prohibiting the privatisation of water and sewage services."

Helda Martinez

In 1993 Colombia legalized privatization of water supplies, allowing companies to sell, distribute, and manage water for a profit. In 2007, 38 percent of the people still had little or no access to clean water, and the Institute of Hydrology, Meteorology and Environmental Studies (IDEAM) predicted that by 2025 that number would rise to 69 percent. In the following viewpoint journalist Helda Martinez asserts that the growing water problem is not due to a lack of water. The United Nations Food and Agriculture Organization (FAO) ranks Colombia seventh in the world for annual renewable freshwater resources. Martinez reports that many Colombians are blaming privatization for the nation's water problems, alleging mismanagement and corruption. In 2007 sixty organizations joined forces to put water management back in the hands of the government via a constitutional amendment and to prohibit privatization. Martinez writes for the Inter

Helda Martinez, "Colombia: Campaign Seeks to Make Water a Constitutional Right," Inter Press Service News Agency, August 24, 2007. Reproduced by permission.

Press Service News Agency (IPS), which is a nonprofit international cooperative of journalists focusing on the needs of the underrepresented in developing nations.

AS YOU READ, CONSIDER THE FOLLOWING QUESTIONS:
1. According to Helda Martinez, where is Colombia ranked in Latin America and in the world in terms of freshwater resources?
2. What does a researcher from one of the NGOs (nongovernmental organizations) in Colombia tell Martinez about the consequences of water privatization in that country?
3. According to Martinez, what pollutes the Bogotá River?

Sixty environmental, indigenous, labour and social organisations in Colombia are carrying out a campaign for a constitutional amendment that would make access to clean water a fundamental right. The proponents of the initiative have already fulfilled the first legal requirement by collecting some 135,000 signatures, equivalent to five out of every 1,000 registered voters. But they now face a bigger challenge.

Once the signatures are certified as valid by the Registraduria Nacional del Estado Civil (national registry), the organizations will have to gain the support of 1.5 million Colombians in order for Congress to call a referendum in which voters would decide in favour of or against the proposed constitutional amendment. The initiative included an awareness-raising caravan along the Magdalena river, which ended Friday when it reached the port of Girardot, 133 km southwest of the capital.

Privatization Is Failing the Poor
In this country of 42 million, nearly 12 million people have no access to clean water and four million have limited access, i.e. to a public faucet, according to the Defensoria del Pueblo (ombudsman's office).

Ironically, Colombia is the second country in Latin America in terms of average annual renewable freshwater resources, and seventh in the world, according to the United Nations Food and Agriculture Organisation (FAO). But despite the abundance, the governmental Institute of Hydrology, Meteorology and Environmental Studies (IDEAM) predicts that 69 percent of the Colombian population will suffer from a lack of clean water in 2025. The non-governmental organisations (NGOs) and trade unions promoting the constitutional amendment point to the privatisation of water utilities, which was authorised by law in 1993, as one of the causes of the problem. "Of the country's 349 water companies, 141 are private and 24 are mixed," reports the CENSAT Agua Viva/Friends of the Earth Colombia.

The amount of fish caught in the Magdalena River in Colombia has dropped almost 90 percent in the last 40 years.

Privatization Drives Up Prices

One of the NGO's researchers, Danilo Urrea, told IPS that "privatisation has significantly driven up the cost of water services, and the granting of concessions to private operators has also given rise to scandals and corruption." In addition, there has been an attempt to charge a toll for navigating the Magdalena river along the stretch where it flows into the Barranquilla port on the Caribbean coast.

The Magdalena river emerges in southwestern Colombia and runs through 18 of the country's 22 departments (provinces) for over 1,500 kilometres before reaching the Caribbean. In the 1970s, 70,000 tons of fish were caught in the river annually, an amount that shrunk to 40,000 in the 1980s, 20,000 in the 1990s and just 8,000 today.

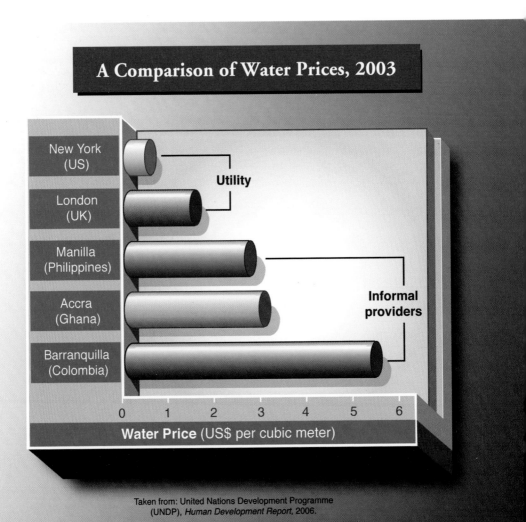

A Comparison of Water Prices, 2003

Utility

Informal providers

New York (US)

London (UK)

Manilla (Philippines)

Accra (Ghana)

Barranquilla (Colombia)

Water Price (US$ per cubic meter)

Taken from: United Nations Development Programme (UNDP), *Human Development Report,* 2006.

That problem is also on the agenda of the groups carrying out the campaign. "You can't just put an end to public utilities arguing that the state is corrupt. What must be achieved is management of water for the benefit of the population as a whole," said Urrea.

Activists Want the Government to Manage Water

The petition drive to collect signatures in favour of the constitutional amendment was launched on May 1 [2007], International Workers' Day, in several cities around Colombia. Various actions were carried out in the following two months, mainly organised by young people. This month [August 2007], during the first forum for water and life in the Caribbean, held in the city of Barranquilla, the caravan set out on the Magdalena river, reaching Girardot on Friday. One of the country's most heavily polluted rivers, the Bogotá river, flows into the Magdalena at the port of Girardot. The Bogotá is a dumping ground for chemical residues from the cut-flower industry and tanneries.

FAST FACT

In 2005 Green Cross International, led by former Soviet leader Mikhail Gorbachev, proposed an international convention on the right to water. Once ratified by the United Nations, it will oblige national governments to make sure that the right to safe water and sanitation is respected.

This first stage of the campaign is coming to a close with "a positive evaluation," said Urrea. "Even if we are not successful in our attempt to hold a referendum, we have carried out awareness-raising efforts in cities and towns along the river, which was part of our overall objective. And of course we will continue working."

Minister of the environment, development and housing Juan Lozano recently stated in a televised debate that he will put a priority on recuperating the country's water resources, and that maintaining a public water service and preserving the environment were aims that he shared.

If a referendum is held and voters come out in favour of a constitutional amendment, Colombia will be following Uruguay's lead. In late 2004, that small South American country became the first nation in the world to introduce a constitutional amendment declaring water resources a public good and prohibiting the privatisation of water and sewage services.

EVALUATING THE AUTHORS' ARGUMENTS:

According to this viewpoint, Colombians have experienced privatization of water for nearly fifteen years, and a group of nongovernmental organizations (NGOs) believes that privatization is doing more harm than good for the poor. Activists want to amend the constitution to place water management back in the hands of the government and prohibit privatization. In the previous viewpoint, Ronald Bailey argues that historically, governments have not adequately provided water for their citizens, catering to the wealthy while neglecting the poor. Compare the two viewpoints. How are proponents of each side (government versus privatization) using the plight of the poor as a means to justify their right to control the water?

Chapter 2

What Common Tools Are Used to Manage Water?

General Motors operations in the Great Lakes region have cut water use, amounting to savings of about 1 billion gallons a year.

Numerous Regulations Are in Place to Increase Dam Safety

"[The National Dam Safety Program] addresses a cross-section of issues and needs, all in support of making U.S. dams safer."

David I. Maurstad

Prior to 1980 no coordinated federal dam safety program and few state laws governed the safety and maintenance of existing dams. In the late 1970s several large dams failed, including Teton Dam, Toccoa Dam, Laurel Run, and Kelly Barnes Dam. The significant loss of life and property prompted President Jimmy Carter to create the Office of Federal Dam Safety in 1980. Eventually this grew to become the National Dam Safety Program (NDSP). In the following viewpoint David I. Maurstad explains that the NDSP promotes dam safety by providing the states with regulations and guidelines, inspector training, research, funding, and information sharing. Maurstad oversees the NDSP as assistant administrator, Mitigation Directorate, in the Department of Homeland Security's Federal Emergency Management Agency (FEMA).

David I. Maurstad, "National Levee and Dam Safety," Statement to U.S. Committee on House Transportation and Infrastructure, May 8, 2007.

AS YOU READ, CONSIDER THE FOLLOWING QUESTIONS:
1. According to this viewpoint, what information does the National Dam Safety Program (NDSP) capture using the 1998 Review Board performance criteria?
2. What is included in NDSP training, according to David I. Maurstad?
3. In Maurstad's view, in what ways are the federally owned dams in the United States significant?

Through grants, training support, research, data collection, and other activities, the [NDSP, or National Dam Safety Program] provides a much needed impetus for the continued safeguarding and protection of people, property, and the dams themselves.

The National Dam Safety Program, which was formally established by Section 215 of the Water Resources and Development Act of 1996 (Public Law 104–303), provides critical support for the operation, maintenance, and improvement of our Nation's dams. The Dam Safety Act of 2006 (Public Law 109–460), which reauthorizes the National Dam Safety Program through Fiscal Year 2011, continues all of the programs established by the 1996 Act.

The NDSP's primary purpose is to provide the States the financial resources they need to strengthen their dam safety programs. The Program supports activities such as: grant assistance to States; State dam safety program improvements; training for State dam safety staff and inspectors; and a technical and archival research program that develops dam safety monitoring devices. The Program also facilitates information exchange between Federal and State dam safety partners through the National Dam Safety Review Board and the Interagency Committee on Dam Safety (ICODS), both of which are chaired by FEMA [Federal Emergency Management Agency].

State Dam Safety Is Supported by the NDSP

According to the 2004–2005 National Dam Safety Biennial Report to Congress, there are approximately 79,500 dams in the United States. The states regulate approximately 95 percent of these. From FY [fiscal year] 2004 through 2007, FEMA distributed a total of approximately

$12.9 million in grant assistance to 49 participating states and Puerto Rico for dam safety.

In 2005, Delaware joined the Program after passing legislation to establish a State dam safety program. The only State not currently participating in the Program is Alabama, which is currently developing the legislation needed to participate in the Program.

Thanks to the recent reauthorization, the National Dam Safety Program continues to improve. Using the Program's 1998 Review Board performance criteria, the NDSP captures information on (1) the state-regulated "high- and significant-hazard potential" dams with Emergency Action Plans (EAPs); (2) the number of dam inspections each State conducts annually; and (3) the dams each State has identified as needing remediation. . . .

Research Ensures Safer Solutions

NDSP research funding addresses a cross-section of issues and needs, all in support of making U.S. dams safer. To guide funding decisions for specific research projects, the National Dam Safety Review Board developed a 5-year Strategic Plan, which ensures that priority is given to research projects that (a) demonstrate a high degree of collaboration and expertise; and (b) will yield products that will contribute to dam safety in the United States.

From a National Security standpoint, the Department of Homeland Security (DHS) is integrating the Review Board's Strategic Plan with the Dam Security Research Plan, which was developed for the Dam Sector Annex to the National Infrastructure Protection Plan.

FAST FACT

Dam building in the United States peaked during the thirty years following World War II, when over one-half of the nation's current total of approximately 79,500 conventional-type dams were built.

Training Equips Dam Safety Professionals

Since the National Dam Safety Program's inception, FEMA has supposed a strong, collaborative training program for dam safety pro-

In 1976 the brand new Teton Dam gave way, causing an estimated $2 billion in damages and eleven deaths. This and other dam failures led to the creation of the National Dam Safety Program.

fessionals and dam owners. Training funds have enabled FEMA to expand training programs, start initiatives to keep pace with evolving technology, and enhance information exchange.

Available at the National, Regional, Local, and even individual "self-paced" levels, NDSP training includes: National Dam Safety Program Technical Workshops on hydrologic deficiencies and potential failure mode analysis and monitoring; the ASDSO Regional Technical Seminars; state training assistance funds; hydrologic modeling system and river analysis system workshops at FEMA's Emergency Management Institute, and the Training Aids for Dam Safety Program.

NDSP is also coordinating with the U.S. Army Corps of Engineers to make training materials available on the Corps Learning Network website . . . , which gives these informative products broad exposure and distribution.

Information Technology Is Critical for Decision-Makers

Technology provides critical tools for the National Dam Safety Program's mission, since an important NDSP objective is to identify, develop, and enhance technology-based tools that can educate the public and help decision-makers.

Important initiatives such as the National Inventory of Dams, the National Performance of Dams Program, and the Dam Safety Program Management Tools system all receive Program funding, allowing them to collect invaluable data on dam status, dam incidents, and dam safety. In turn, this information helps National Dam Safety Program partners effectively document failure modes and identify critical research and training needs.

Federal Guidelines Improve Safety and Security

Although the Federal Government owns or regulates only about five percent of the dams in the United States, many of these facilities are significant in terms of size, function, public benefit, and hazard potential. Since the implementation of the Federal Guidelines for Dam Safety, the Federal agencies responsible for these dams have made significant strides in ensuring the safety of dams within their jurisdictions.

All of the federal agencies responsible for dams have implemented the Federal Guidelines. Many of the agencies maintain comprehensive training programs as well as research and development programs, and have even incorporated security considerations into these efforts to protect their dams against terrorist threats.

In addition, Federal-State cooperation and coordination has increased in many areas, such as emergency action planning, inspection, research and development, training, and information exchange.

Dam Security Is Improved by Collaboration

Dam safety and dam security are complementary programs, and collaboration between dam sector stakeholders certainly will continue. For example, FEMA coordinates with the DHS Risk Management Division, the Sector Specific Agency for the Dam Sector. We fully

Dam Ownership in the United States

Although most infrastructure facilities, such as roads, bridges, and sewer systems, are owned by public entities, the majority of dams in the United States are privately owned. Dam owners are responsible for the safety, upkeep, and repair of the dams.

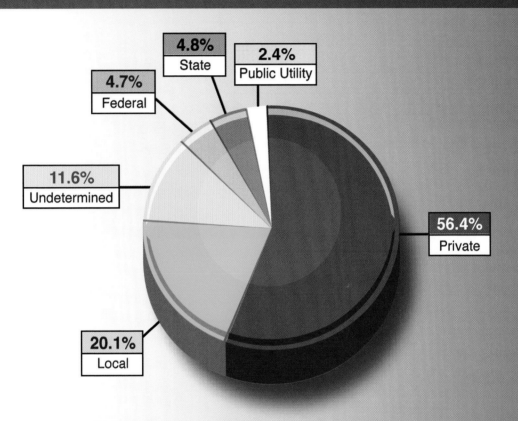

Taken from: National Inventory of Dams, February 2005. Available at http://www.fema.gov.

support and will participate in the framework established by the National Infrastructure Protection Plan, including the Government Coordinating Council (GCC) and the Sector Coordinating Council (SCC), and the GCC Workgroups.

There is significant cross-representation of the federal and state professionals involved in dam safety and dam security. These professionals serve on the DHS-chaired groups, as well as the FEMA-NDSP-chaired groups, including the National Dam Safety Review Board and the Interagency Committee on Dam Safety. FEMA's continued participation on the GCC and in support of the Sector Coordinating Council will facilitate the ability of both groups to address critical issues of common concern.

EVALUATING THE AUTHOR'S ARGUMENTS:

In this viewpoint David I. Maurstad cites numerous regulations, programs, and initiatives that are designed to improve dam safety in the United States. In his role in the Federal Emergency Management Agency (FEMA), Maurstad oversees the National Dam Safety Program (NDSP). Do his position in the government and his listing of government programs make for a more compelling argument than if he worked for a private or nonprofit organization? Why or why not?

Viewpoint

2

Regulated Dams Remain Unsafe

Gaylord Shaw

"Every moment of every day, unsafe dams form a vast reservoir of danger throughout America."

In the following viewpoint Gaylord Shaw acknowledges that federal and state regulations under the National Dam Safety Program have helped to identify thousands of unsafe dams. These deteriorating dams, often originally built in sparsely populated areas, are now looming over densely populated communities. Shaw argues that more is needed than laws and regulations to make dams safe; states need money and manpower to enforce existing laws and to facilitate dam repairs. Shaw, a journalist, has devoted much of his career to studying and writing about the problems of dam safety. He earned a Pulitzer prize in 1978 for his reporting on unsafe dams.

AS YOU READ, CONSIDER THE FOLLOWING QUESTIONS:
1. According to the author, what serious dam problem confronts the residents of Denver, Colorado?
2. In Shaw's view, what sets President Jimmy Carter apart from recent U.S. presidents in terms of dam safety?
3. While nearly every state now has dam safety laws, what does Shaw describe as a persistent problem for U.S. dams?

The landscape of America, at last count, is dotted with 79,272 large dams [as of January 2006]. Most of them safely deliver bountiful benefits—trillions of gallons of water for drinking, irrigation, and industrial use, plus flood control, recreation, hydroelectric power, and navigation.

That's the good news. Here, in my opinion, is the bad news: Disaster lurks in thousands of those dams.

At least 3,500 of America's big dams are unsafe, according to inspection reports filed away in obscure nooks and crannies of government offices across the country. Thousands more dams also are unsafe, the American Society of Civil Engineers concluded this year, but no one knows for certain how many because few states have the funds for even cursory safety inspections.

Thus, every moment of every day, unsafe dams form a vast reservoir of danger throughout America. That's not an overstatement. I'm not a professional engineer, but I've spent nearly two-thirds of my 45-year career in journalism studying unsafe dams. I've done on-the-scene reporting on dam failures that killed 175 people and caused billions of dollars in property damage. I've interviewed scores of victims, dozens of state and federal engineers, inspectors, and officials, and examined records on hundreds of dams.

In my view, the cumulative hazard posed by unsafe dams is huge, but it remains largely unexplored by the media. When a dam fails—and records suggest dozens do each year—the events usually are viewed as local, transitory incidents rather than a symbol of a national problem.

Man-Made Structures Can Fail

Hurricane Katrina underscored the peril of depending on man-made structures for protection against disaster. Failure of the New Orleans levee system during the storm this year contributed to prolonged flooding and 1,300 deaths.

Months later, as scenes of misery and dislocation lingered in the public mind, President [George W.] Bush urgently asked Congress to approve $3 billion for the Army Corps of Engineers to begin rebuilding New Orleans' battered levees. The House of Representatives included that amount in a $29 billion hurricane recovery assistance package it passed three days later.

In concept and construction, levees are close cousins of dams. But while politicians flocked to support repair of New Orleans' levees, they've virtually ignored a proposed Dam Rehabilitation and Repair Act which has languished for nearly a year in a House subcommittee. The proposal would authorize the Federal Emergency Management Agency (FEMA) to disperse $350 million over four years to help states repair unsafe dams. Chances of Congress enacting such a repair program anytime soon are slim.

Floodwater is held back by Ohio's Dover Dam, one of the country's most at-risk dams, but a large flood could cause it to fail.

It Will Cost Billions to Repair Unsafe Dams

The $350 million program would be a down payment of less than 10 percent toward the estimated $36.2 billion total cost of repairing America's unsafe dams. It also is approximately one-eighth of the amount the president is seeking for repair of the New Orleans levees.

This is not to suggest that the New Orleans levees go unrepaired. But from New England to Hawaii more and more aging dams are experiencing problems, with little public awareness. A few large and small examples:

- Taunton, Mass., got national attention in October [2005] when a 173-year-old, 12-foot-tall wooden dam above its business district began to buckle. Stores and schools were closed for a week and townspeople headed for higher ground. The crisis eased when the water level behind the dam was lowered. The federal government is now paying 75 percent of the $189,410 cost of tearing down Whittenton Mills Dam and replacing it with a new one.

- In the placid Schoharie River Valley of upstate New York, a volunteer group calling itself Dam Concerned Citizens was formed [in December 2005] to press for emergency repairs to 182-foot-tall Gilboa Dam, built 80 years ago to supply drinking water to New York City. The dam has been leaking for years. Now citizens have established their own website which distributes emergency notification plans and publicizes preselected evacuation routes for use should the dam fail.

- Residents of Denver, Colo., population 2 million plus, were warned [in December 2005] by the [U.S. Army] Corps of Engineers that serious safety problems have been detected at Cherry Creek Dam, a 141-foot-tall earthen structure. The dam was built 55 years ago on what was then windswept pastureland 10 miles south of Denver. Now the dam looms above Interstate 225, a cluster of office parks and swank homes, a nationally known golf course, and several schools.

The National Dam Safety Program Is Aware of the Problem

Bruce Tschantz, professor emeritus at the University of Tennessee who 25 years ago helped establish the first Office of Dam Safety [which developed into the National Dam Safety Program] in the then-nascent FEMA, reached back into classical mythology to fetch a phrase—"the sword of Damocles"—to express his concern about the dangers posed by deficient dams perched above developed areas. (Damocles was a courtier at the court of Dionysius 1 in the 4th century BC. He was so gushing in his praise of the power and happiness of Dionysius that the tyrant, to illustrate the precariousness of rank and power, gave a banquet and had a sword suspended above the head of Damocles by a single hair.)

"We know what the problems are, we know where they are, and we know how to fix them," Dr. Tschantz said in a telephone interview. It's that next step—actually getting the money to fix them—where we're stalled."

Tschantz doesn't point fingers of blame. But it's clear to me that Congress and several presidents, including the current occupant of the White House [George W. Bush], share culpability on the national level, and that too many state and local officials have grown weary of trying to find sources of financing to make dams safer.

Disaster Led to Government Action

Jimmy Carter was the last president to display serious and sustained interest in the issue. He had been in office less than a year when, in the early morning darkness of a Sunday in November 1977, a never-inspected dam in the mountains of his home state of Georgia collapsed and sent a wall of water crashing down upon the campus of Toccoa Falls Bible College—a campus he had visited several times.

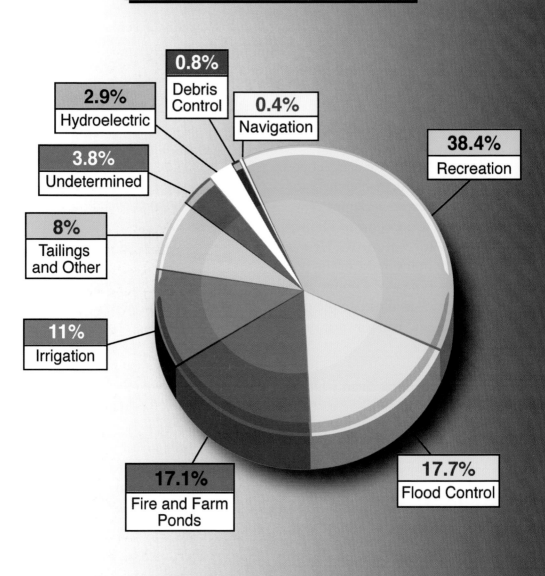

Dams Provide Many Benefits

0.8% Debris Control

2.9% Hydroelectric

0.4% Navigation

38.4% Recreation

3.8% Undetermined

8% Tailings and Other

11% Irrigation

17.1% Fire and Farm Ponds

17.7% Flood Control

Taken from: National Inventory of Dams, February 2005. Available at http://www.fema.gov.

The Kelly Barnes Dam on Toccoa Creek dated back to 1899, when a rock-and-timber structure was built across a fast-flowing mountain stream to impound water for a small hydroelectric plant. Later, Toccoa Falls Bible Institute chose the valley below as the site for its campus, took over the power plant and, in 1937, decided to construct an earthen embankment over the original dam, eventually raising the structure's height to 42 feet.

Neglected Dams Are Dangerous

Twenty years later, in 1957, the school abandoned the power plant. For the next two decades, the dam was neglected, visited only by an occasional fisherman or hiker. Pine trees grew to maturity on its downstream slope, sending roots deep into the dam's core. Portions of the steep embankment vanished in a landslide, but there were no repairs, even though water seeped almost continuously from the base of the dam. Finally, the weakened 78-year-old dam collapsed during a rainy night in Georgia.

In the valley below, Eldon Elsberry and two friends were on patrol in the campus fire department's Jeep. When the wall of water hit, it overturned the vehicle. "One minute the water [in the creek] was inches deep, and the next I was swimming for my life," Mr. Elsberry said. "I saw the bank and made for it." He turned and saw one of his friends struggling in the water. "I reached for his hand. He went by so fast I couldn't touch him."

Experts later calculated that the water released by the dam's collapse weighed approximately the same as 7,500 locomotives. As the water crashed across the campus, it destroyed a dormitory and crushed a cluster of mobile homes where married students lived.

States Need More Money

Later, in the mud and tangled debris, 39 bodies were found. Twenty were children. College officials said they never hired a private consulting engineer because they had no idea it had safety problems. The state of Georgia never inspected the dam because, at the time, there was no state law requiring such inspections. Few other states had dam safety laws then, either. Pennsylvania was one of the exceptions. Its tough law was spurred by memories of the 1889 collapse of South Fork Dam above Johnstown that killed 2,209 people. Yet even with the strong state law requiring regular safety inspections, another 55 people in the same community died in July 1977 after the failure of Laurel Run Dam, just a few miles from where South Fork Dam triggered the disaster 88 years earlier.

While all states except Alabama now have laws or regulations establishing dam safety programs, enforcement is spotty, largely because of the paucity of inspectors. In Texas, for example, there are only six state employees to inspect nearly 7,500 dams. One Texas official noted that with the current staff level "some dams would not be examined for three centuries."

Let's do the math. Two of my teenaged grandchildren live in Texas. If we count 30 years for each generation, that means all the dams in Texas will be inspected by the time my grandchildren's great-great-great-great-great-great-great-great-great-grandchildren ring in a new year in 2306. Reassuring isn't it?

EVALUATING THE AUTHORS' ARGUMENTS:

In the previous viewpoint the author describes the numerous programs and initiatives that promote dam safety. In this viewpoint the author employs human-interest anecdotes to demonstrate that dams are unsafe. Which viewpoint do you feel makes a more persuasive argument? Cite examples from the viewpoints to support your position.

Lawn Watering Restrictions Are Effective

Jason Hardin

"Water use dropped from 46.2 million gallons . . . to 40.5 million."

The city of Greensboro, North Carolina, was built around railroad lines rather than a natural water source such as a river, and its water supply is limited. In 2007, due to a prolonged drought, city officials opted to add a lawn-watering restriction to its water resource policy. The restrictions were mandatory and enforced by city employees. In the following viewpoint Jason Hardin examines the city's efforts to enforce the restrictions. He reports that water use did not drop as much as the city had hoped, but that the difference was still significant. Hardin is a staff writer for the *News & Record* of Greensboro.

AS YOU READ, CONSIDER THE FOLLOWING QUESTIONS:
1. According to this viewpoint, how can an observer tell the difference between watered and unwatered lawns when looking down from above?
2. How did city employees at the water resources headquarters prepare to enforce the new water restrictions in Greensboro?
3. According to Hardin, to what level does water demand need to drop in order for the city to meet its goal?

Jeff Denny cruises slowly along a suburban street, looking for law-breakers. Suddenly, he spots evidence of something amiss and pulls his big Chevy truck to the side.

"Right here," he says. "You can see it on the driveway." Water. Busted.

The City Enforces Its Restrictions

Wednesday [August 29, 2007] marked the first day that city employees began actively enforcing Greensboro's new mandatory water restrictions, which took effect Monday. That meant no sprinklers,

Some people believe that imposing lawn watering restrictions will help save significant amounts of water during droughts.

and no exceptions. Enforcers don't even need to catch someone red-handed with a sprinkler running—evidence that they had been on earlier, running through the night, is enough.

Armed with a clipboard and a large cup of McDonald's coffee, Denny made his way through the city's greenest neighborhoods. His eyes scanned the streets for the telltale signs of sprinklers that had been in use: half-moons of wet pavement, mulch of varying colors. Finding violators wasn't hard. In less than four hours of crisscrossing residential streets, Denny racked up more than 50 citations.

> ## FAST FACT
>
> The average American uses nearly 100 gallons of water daily for preparing food, bathing, washing clothes and dishes, flushing toilets, and watering lawns and gardens.

Spotting Violators Is Easy

"I know the neighborhoods," he said. "I know where they would be watering."

The difference in watered and unwatered lawns can be startling. From above, the suburbs must look like a giant checkerboard, with lush green squares alternating with yellowish-brown yards.

At times, Denny found violations as fast as he could write them down. "It's just sad," he said. "A lot of folks, I'm sure, are oblivious. A lot of folks, I'm sure, don't care."

But others do.

Residents Police Their Neighbors

By Wednesday afternoon, residents had informed the city of well more than 100 properties they suspected of illegally irrigating this week, said Kristine Williams of the city's water resources department. Some were quite enthusiastic. "We had somebody fax us a list of all their neighbors who were irrigating," she said.

Tips aren't the only tool the city is using to pinpoint the locations of illicit sprinklers. The day before Denny began his sweep, Kenny Treadway sat at a desk in the water resources headquarters on South Elm-Eugene Street, looking at maps. Treadway was putting together

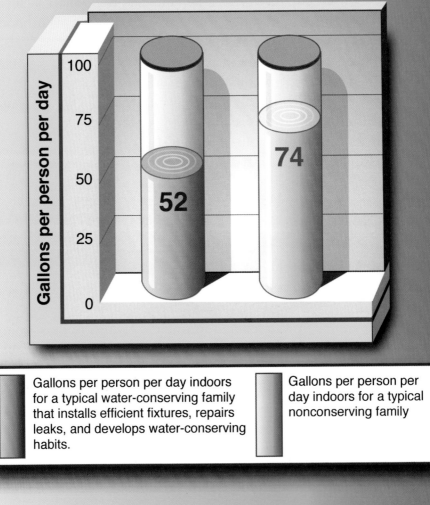

Typical Indoor Water Use in Greensboro, North Carolina

Gallons per person per day

100

75

50

25

0

52

74

Gallons per person per day indoors for a typical water-conserving family that installs efficient fixtures, repairs leaks, and develops water-conserving habits.

Gallons per person per day indoors for a typical nonconserving family

Taken from: Greensboro Water Resources. www.greensboro-nc.gov.

a map aimed at highlighting areas where violations might be likely, based on the location of irrigation meters. That, along with maps that show areas of heavy use, helps take the guesswork out of enforcement, city officials say. "We know where there's a lot of irrigation going on," Williams said.

It's too early to judge the impact of the mandatory restrictions, but demand has dropped in recent days, she said.

Water Use Has Dropped

Water use dropped from 46.2 million gallons last Tuesday to 40.5 million two days ago, she said. That's still too high, however. Water officials say the demand needs to drop to the mid-30s to stem the bleeding.

Because the voluntary restrictions didn't work, Denny and others will continue to hit the streets. He doesn't mind the work. In fact, he's happy to help.

"If everyone would do their part, we would . . . be in better shape," he said. "It's the law. Technically, they're lawbreakers."

EVALUATING THE AUTHOR'S ARGUMENTS:

According to the author, just three days after the city of Greensboro implemented its mandatory water restrictions, it sent out paid enforcers to ticket violators. That same afternoon residents began voluntarily submitting the names of their neighbors whom they suspected of violating the restriction. In your opinion, what are the pros and cons of citizens policing fellow citizens in a community? Give reasons for your answers.

Viewpoint 4

Lawn Watering Restrictions Are Not Effective

Sarah Lindenfeld Hall and Sam LaGrone

"One expert said alternate-day watering schedules . . . have little impact."

During the summer of 2007, like many areas in the South, Raleigh, North Carolina, was experiencing drought conditions. With little rain to replenish Falls Lake—the source of the city's drinking water—experts predicted that the lake would dry out by January 2008. On July 2 city officials instituted mandatory restrictions on lawn watering to conserve water. In the following viewpoint Sarah Lindenfeld Hall and Sam LaGrone report that during the month following the mandatory restrictions, instead of finding a decrease in water consumption, city officials found that several new daily records for water consumption were set. Lindenfeld and LaGrone indicate that city officials then considered further restrictions and rate hikes as well as improved education about conservation. Hall and LaGrone are staff writers for the *News & Observer*.

AS YOU READ, CONSIDER THE FOLLOWING QUESTIONS:
1. According to this viewpoint, what did Raleigh Public Utilities director Dale Crisp admit?
2. According to Crisp, why did he decide to toughen restrictions?
3. What did a study of western cities show to be the most effective water-reduction program?

D espite mandatory restrictions, Raleigh's water use has soared this month [August 2007] setting three all-time daily highs.

The use directly correlates with recording-breaking temperatures. Still, the numbers startled city officials, because use spiked when only half of their water customers should have been watering their lawns, which officials think accounts for as much as 20 percent of total water consumption.

One expert said alternate-day watering schedules such as Raleigh's—which will become more restrictive Tuesday—have little impact. And a City Council member thinks the city needs to do still more.

The City Made a Mistake

Raleigh Public Utilities Director Dale Crisp admitted Thursday [August 23, 2007] that the city might have erred by not limiting the times of day when people could water lawns.

"To be under the restrictions when those records were set made it more surprising," Crisp said. "Now we know that not everyone has complied with those."

Falls Lake, the city's source of drinking water, which is about 4 feet below normal, would dry out Jan. 6 [2008] unless customers cut their use or the area gets substantial rain.

The city has issued nearly 500 warnings and fines since mandatory restrictions went into effect July 2. Today, the city will turn off the water

> **FAST FACT**
>
> For over five years, Cary, North Carolina, has piped up to 5 million gallons of reclaimed water per day to homes and businesses. Reclaimed water is treated domestic water that is unsuitable for drinking water, but safe for irrigation and cooling.

at a new home in North Raleigh's Bedford community because the builder didn't follow the rules, despite a warning and two fines totaling $250.

The City Will Increase Restrictions

On Tuesday, the city will limit lawn watering with sprinklers and irrigation systems to one day a week and vehicle and power washing to the weekends.

The restrictions extend to all the city's water customers, including those in Garner, Rolesville, Wake Forest, Knightdale, Wendell and Zebulon. Those customers, on top of Raleigh's growing population base, have helped to strain the system, City Council member Philip Isley said.

"We're essentially providing water for most of the county, and that obviously puts strain on our infrastructure," Isley said.

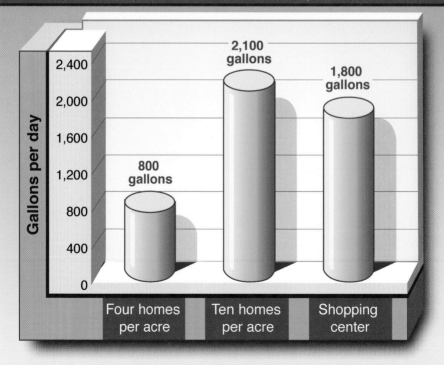

Development Determines Water Consumption

The city of Raleigh, North Carolina, estimates how much water will be consumed by the development of one acre of land–based on how the land is developed.

Taken from: Sarah Lindenfeld Hall, "Raleigh to Review Growth, Water," *News & Observer* (Raleigh, NC), May 23, 2006.

Some claim that lawn watering restrictions haven't effectively stemmed water use during serious drought conditions in North Carolina.

The Long-Term Forecast Looks Bleak

Crisp said he decided on the tougher restrictions this week after a long-term forecast from state officials Tuesday said the drought conditions would remain for three to six months. Forecasters said conditions are similar to a drought in the 1940s when significant rain didn't come until late February—more than a month after Falls Lake is expected to run out of water. "We've got to change that paradigm," Crisp said.

Ari M. Michelsen, director of the Texas A&M University's Agricultural Research and Extension Center at El Paso, said alternate-day watering restrictions usually aren't effective. "They tend to water more on the day that they can water," he said.

Michelsen was part of a team of water researchers that evaluated several Western cities to find the most effective water-saving strategies. They found that regulation alone will, on average, reduce water usage by 3 percent.

There Is a Better Way

The study said the most effective water-reduction programs combined water-conservation education, encouraging the use of water-efficient faucets and shower heads and giving incentives to purchase water-saving appliances.

Raleigh's water-conservation task force recommended some of those measures in a report a year ago, along with new rates that encourage conservation. City Council members balked at some of them, calling them too expensive, difficult to enforce or having little effect. The task force also recommended limiting the time when people could water, but the city ultimately set no limit.

Crisp said Thursday that might have been a mistake. Some people are heeding the restrictions but watering for a long time on the days irrigation is allowed.

City Council member Thomas Crowder said the city needs to do a better job. He'd like to see the city capture the water when it flushes fire hydrants or water lines to use to irrigate its parks. And he has proposed setting a tiered rate system where people who use the most water would pay at higher rates.

EVALUATING THE AUTHORS' ARGUMENTS:

In this viewpoint the authors cite examples to show that some people in Raleigh do not care about the water problem. For instance, water consumption hit a record high on a day when only 50 percent of the people could legally water their lawns, and one builder kept breaking the water-restriction law even though he received a warning and two fines. City officials in Raleigh have considered raising the water rates to curtail water use. The author of the previous viewpoint indicated that in Greensboro, North Carolina, numerous residents voluntarily informed city officials of neighbors who violated water restrictions. In your opinion, how can city officials balance their tools of restriction, raised rates, and citizen enforcement, while being fair to all the citizens? Please cite examples and give reasons for your answers.

Reclaiming Wetlands Is Easy

WaterMarks

*"**Vegetation is one of the easiest coastal restoration projects to do'**.... 'You've just got to get out there quick and plant.'"*

Louisiana is home to 40 percent—3 million acres—of the nation's continental wetlands. These fragile lands purify water, preserve shoreline by absorbing water wave energy, and create wildlife habitat. Due to human activity and the natural effects of wind and wave action, Louisiana is struggling to maintain existing and to reclaim former wetland areas. In the following viewpoint the authors discuss three successful wetland reclamation projects. For each project, specific native vegetation was hand-planted to jump-start the stabilization of at-risk areas. According to this viewpoint, using vegetation to reclaim wetlands is not only easy, it also results in long-term stabilization of the habitat. *WaterMarks* is published three times a year by the Louisiana Coastal Wetlands Conservation and Restoration Taskforce to communicate news and issues of interest related to the Coastal Wetlands Planning, Protection, and Restoration Act of 1990.

"Successful Projects Reclaim Wetlands: Vegetative Plantings Take Hold," *WaterMarks*, April 2005, pp. 8–10. Reproduced by permission.

With the state losing land at the rate of a football field about every half-hour, the news about Louisiana's wetlands is often dire.

As a means of stemming that loss and reclaiming marsh habitat, vegetative plantings offer a solid basis for hope.

"Vegetation is one of the easiest coastal restoration projects to do," says Kenneth Bahlinger, landscape architect with the Louisiana Department of Natural Resources (DNR). "You've just got to get out there quick and plant."

Hand Planting Is Important

Revegetation may occur naturally, Bahlinger explains, but in many instances that won't happen before tides, storms, boat wakes, and other forces of erosion wash away sediment. Hand plantings can jump-start natural vegetation growth, creating a more stable home for plants and animals.

Three recent projects—on Queen Bess Island, in the Sabine National Wildlife Refuge and at Boston Canal/Vermilion Bay— illustrate this premise and the potential plants have for holding on to Louisiana's land.

Plants Create Habitat

The success of Queen Bess Island, Bahlinger says, is easy to see: "Just count the birds. That island is full of pelicans."

Twenty years ago the brown pelican, Louisiana's state bird, had vanished from Louisiana's coastal wetlands as DDT [a synthetic insecticide] pollution endangered its young and erosion claimed its habitat. Following a national ban on the use of DDT, the state reintroduced pelicans from Florida and began re-establishing their habitat. In the Barataria Bay Waterway Wetland Creation project, sediment dredged from the waterway was placed on Queen Bess Island. This small island in the Barataria-Terrebonne Estuary System [BTES] had lost nearly two-thirds of its land due to storms, erosion from boat wakes, and lack of vegetation.

Hand Planting Helped Pelicans

One factor in the pelican's remarkable recovery—from just 675 nests in the BTES in 1990 to more than 6,500 in 2001—was the "greening" of Queen Bess: the hand planting of two plant species. Black mangrove trees now provide nesting areas for the pelicans, while smooth cordgrass collects sediment and serves as habitat for fish and crustaceans.

"What we've planted there has spread and covered Queen Bess," Bahlinger says. "Those plants are actually helping hold sediment on the island. The plants are thriving, and so are the pelicans."

Seaside heliotrope is planted at the edge of the Ballona Wetlands in the Marina del Rey area of Los Angeles.

A Marsh Is Reclaimed

The Sabine National Wildlife Refuge—an ecotourism attraction and educational resource that draws some 300,000 visitors each year—is part of a vast ecosystem between the Calcasieu and Sabine rivers. But the construction of the Calcasieu Ship Channel in the 1960s, along with natural forces such as hurricanes, increased salinity in much of the marsh, killing its native plants and converting portions of it to open water.

To re-establish Sabine's wetlands, one recent project (Sabine Refuge Marsh Creation, Cycle 1) created marsh from open water areas by building temporary earthen containment dikes, then filling the areas between them with material dredged from the Calcasieu Ship Channel. The perimeter of the area and the edges of trenasses—man-made bayous permitting the natural movement of water and wildlife—were planted with smooth cordgrass, which holds the sediment in place and helps create a functioning marsh as it spreads to the interior of the dredged material.

Hand Planting Keeps Soil in Place

"Vegetation would probably have eventually covered the created areas naturally," says Leigh Anne Sharp, coastal scientist with the DNR. "But hand plantings made it happen faster because it kept the soil in place."

Four more cycles of pumping of dredged material are planned for other areas in the refuge, but results are already positive.

"The plants filled in really quickly and are beginning to create the marsh habitat," says Sharp. "This area is ripe for restoration. The cells of marsh we're building should help save the entire refuge."

Reclaiming the Shoreline

For decades, wind-driven waves pounding the shoreline of Vermilion Bay and wakes from boats traveling into Boston Canal scoured away soil and plants from the fragile wetlands bordering the bay.

"Once the shoreline eroded back far enough, the open water areas within those wetlands would become part of Vermilion Bay and the interior marshland would be lost," says Cindy Steyer, coastal vegetative specialist with the Natural Resources Conservation Service (NRCS).

As part of the 1995 Boston Canal/Vermilion Bay Shoreline Protection project, the NRCS and DNR planted 35,000 "Vermilion" smooth cordgrass transplants along a 14-mile stretch of Vermilion Bay shoreline. The goal: to dissipate wave energy to reduce the rate of shoreline erosion.

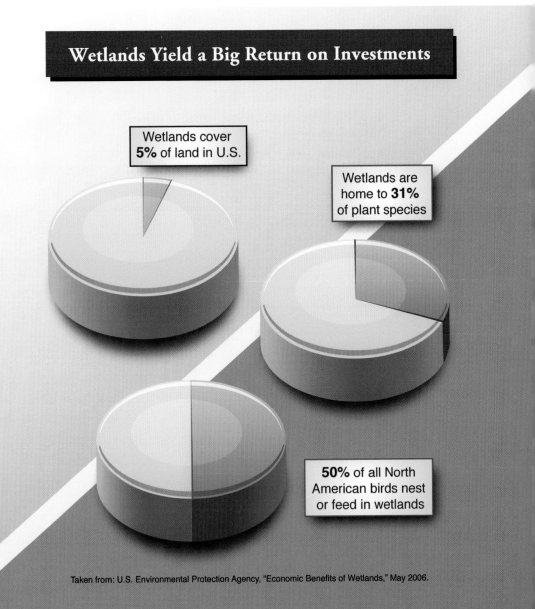

Wetlands Yield a Big Return on Investments

Wetlands cover **5%** of land in U.S.

Wetlands are home to **31%** of plant species

50% of all North American birds nest or feed in wetlands

Taken from: U.S. Environmental Protection Agency, "Economic Benefits of Wetlands," May 2006.

Ten years later, the cordgrass has not only stabilized the shoreline, it is also collecting sediment, creating marsh that other native plants have begun to colonize naturally.

"We hoped the smooth cordgrass would just slow the rate of shoreline loss," Steyer says. "But it has exceeded our expectations by actually promoting shoreline gain."

EVALUATING THE AUTHORS' ARGUMENTS:

According to this viewpoint, different human activities hastened the loss of each of the three wetlands being reclaimed. Scientists are now hand-planting these restored areas to hasten their restoration. However, a DNR coastal scientist is quoted in the viewpoint as saying, "Vegetation would probably have eventually covered the created areas naturally." In your opinion, does this viewpoint demonstrate the value of spending time and money to hasten a recovery that will probably happen naturally? Give reasons for your answer.

Reclaiming Wetlands Can Be Difficult

"We're facing the biggest public-works project in the history of the city. You're basically retrofitting a city that was developed in the wrong way."

Judith Lewis

Los Angeles is commonly known as a desert community. Almost all of its native creeks, streams, and rivers have been run underground and paved over. The resulting hardscape has led to urban runoff—pollutants like lawn fertilizer and nonbiodegradable litter that are washed into waterways—which is California's biggest source of water pollution. In the following viewpoint Judith Lewis explains that some experts are now recommending that Los Angeles go to great lengths to reclaim its wetlands, which will, in turn, allow the sun, soil, and vegetation to clean water the natural way. Lewis describes the abundant challenges Los Angeles would face in this effort. Lewis, an award-winning author, writes on environmental issues for *LA Weekly* magazine.

AS YOU READ, CONSIDER THE FOLLOWING QUESTIONS:

1. According to this viewpoint, what is the principal reason Southern Californians hate water?
2. According to Rex Frankel, cited in this viewpoint, what are the three options Los Angeles has for cleaning up its pollution?
3. What would the city of Los Angeles have to do to restore its rivers, in Frankel's view?

Judith Lewis, "The Lost Streams of Los Angeles," *LA Weekly*, November 8, 2006. Reproduced by permission.

Throughout the world, engineers have tried to constrain rivers, freeze them in their paths and contain them in their banks, but no one disappeared creeks more efficiently than the people who built Los Angeles. In many other large cities, free-running creeks are something to construct a little paradise around—the desirable "water features" touted in so many development brochures. Here in Southern California, streams are regarded as a nuisance—ditches in the summertime that flood in heavy rains. We run them underground, pave them over and move them aside to install our pools or build our new housing and construct our retail developments.

"We are absolutely unique in that way," says Mark Gold, executive director of Heal the Bay. "The rest of the country laughs when they see what we've done. For Southern California, a stream seems to be a concrete trapezoidal channel."

Then again, in those other places, little brooks and big rivers babble and flow pretty much all year round. The streams of Los Angeles, taking a cue from the river they feed into, can't be trusted to shimmer with water for even half the year. In this land of meteorological mood swings, many creek beds turn to dusty ravines for several months, and then roar to life during winter rains, rising far beyond their banks and sometimes messing with the landscape by carving out new routes. In retribution for their inconstancy, Los Angeles has wiped out 94 percent of its streams, creeks and rivers. And we're trying to get rid of the rest.

Even as efforts to restore the Los Angeles River have become uncontroversially hip, efforts to divert, channelize and drain the Santa Clara River, just 30 miles north, have accelerated. A housing development along its banks, ironically named Riverpark, will require that the Santa Clara's banks be stabilized with rock and concrete; a cement mining operation scheduled for the river's upper reaches will deplete the aquifer that feeds its springs along its only perennial stretch.

Wetlands Purify Water

This has consequences that go beyond aesthetics. City planners and architects now understand that streams and wetlands are excellent cleaning agents. By slowing, spreading and sinking water before it has a chance to reach the ocean, they allow sunlight and soil to act as a

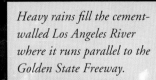

Heavy rains fill the cement-walled Los Angeles River where it runs parallel to the Golden State Freeway.

natural water-treatment system: The sun's ultraviolet light helps kill viruses; soil filters bacteria. Cattails and other wetland plants take up nitrogen and other nutrients.

Had [Los Angeles'] streams not been turned into fast-moving concrete channels and storm drains . . . , Southern California's beaches would never have suffered from the pollution that blights them today. Instead, the toxic accumulation of our lives—our fertilizer, our dogs' poop, our plastic wrappers—speeds down our streets and through our storm drains toward the sea, only to wash up on our beaches every rainy winter. It also trickles down to the coasts in the summer and shows up in the depleted aquifers that some municipalities depend on for a fraction of their drinking water. Health officials close beaches in Los Angeles County twice as often as they do anywhere else in the country, and the people who monitor beach water quality increasingly target "dry-weather runoff" as a cause of summertime illnesses among surfers and swimmers.

"The biggest source of water pollution in California is urban runoff," says David Beckman of the Natural Resources Defense Council. . . .

Los Angeles Had Dangerous Floods

The principal reason Southern Californians hate water: Back when the Los Angeles River was lined with willows, Watts and Compton were marshland and Inglewood was "coastal prairie" (the reason a major thoroughfare bisecting the city from north to south is called "Prairie"), homes, farms and even people were regularly lost to the water.

Los Angeles used to be a land of catastrophic floods. One of the most devastating was the big flood of 1938, after which the U.S. Army Corps of Engineers stepped in to turn the Los Angeles River into the concrete channel it is today. Most Angelenos who complain about the concrete don't know how often floods happened here, and not just along the big river's banks: In 1811, 1815, 1822, 1825, 1832, 1842, 1852, 1858 and 1859, Los Angeles County flooded

> ## FAST FACT
>
> A 1902 federal map of the Los Angeles basin shows abundant streams, most of which were filled in and paved over by the end of the twentieth century.

in various places from its southern reaches to the Santa Monica Mountains; in the winters of 1861–62, 1867–68, 1888–89 and 1914, those floods were disastrous. They ripped up buildings and swept away crops and cattle. They made it possible to sail from San Pedro to Compton, and impossible to travel over ground from Compton to Los Angeles. . . .

The City Has Three Options

Few know better how hard it is to unpave paradise than Rex Frankel. As director of the Ballona Ecosystem Education Project, he has long fought—futilely, in some respects—to preserve the Ballona Wetlands, 90 percent of which has been compromised by development. He has come to realize that the Ballona Wetlands' health would improve if the county and city could fix the urban-runoff problem. And so he has also worked hard to put together the numbers to demonstrate that daylighting creeks [unearthing buried waterways] and restoring wetlands may actually make financial, as well as environmental, sense.

The way Frankel sees it, Los Angeles has three options available to it for cleaning up pollution caused by urban runoff. It can install small-scale systems that capture as much pollution as possible close to its source—filtration devices that either stop garbage from flowing downstream or divert water to existing parks where it can percolate into the ground. "That's the city's one," says Frankel. "They think it's the cheap way of doing it."

The second option, also proposed in the city of Los Angeles' Integrated Resource Plan, is to divert the water to regional treatment plants, facilities that will treat urban runoff like sewage, and cleanse it of nutrients before it hits the beach. "And the third way," he says, "is to unpave our rivers as much as possible, acquire any potential vacant land along the rivers and use them as part of an expanded green-space network."

A Greenway System Would Help

Frankel, a boyish-looking 42-year-old, almost always dressed in short-sleeved shirts and shorts, sits in his office on L.A.'s Westside where the walls are lined with maps—maps of the Los Angeles basin, of the

Ballona Watershed, of a proposed greenway system that would connect all of the local area's open space with contiguous parks, daylighted streams and restored wetlands. "You can't stop the public from doing dumb things," he says as he talks about the reasons individual efforts, though crucial, aren't enough to solve our pollution problem. "Our existence every day produces trash and pollution, and the most concerned citizen can't always prevent it. You need a system that's fail-safe to deal with it. You can't count on education; you've got to have the infrastructure. And it's going to be incredibly expensive to do it either of the first two ways."

The first option is based on the city's proposal to use some 30 publicly owned sites to reclaim water and use it for landscape irrigation around the region of Los Angeles known as the Santa Monica Bay Watershed—Venice, the Los Angeles Airport area, Pacific Palisades and El Segundo, from which all runoff drains into the ocean. It's a nice idea, says Frankel, but according to his calculations, "They were only capturing about 2 percent of the runoff that the city says it needs cleaned up to meet Clean Water Act standards. The number of days they'd violate health regulations wouldn't decrease at all."

It's Important to Fund the Right Project

By the city's own estimates, the project will cost $30 million. "If that's $30 million to clean up only 2 percent of the runoff," says Frankel, "that means you have to multiply that $30 million by 50 to get 100 percent compliance [with EPA standards]." On top of that, the Santa Monica Bay Watershed constitutes only 10 percent of the land area in the city of L.A. "So you have to multiply that cost by 10," says Frankel. "That means that to enact this plan for the whole city would cost $15 billion."

Treatment plants, he estimates, could come to $15 billion too. "It's not just the treatment plants," he says, "it's getting the water to the treatment plants. You have to do a lot of digging up of old systems and building new ones." An underground water tank, or cistern, costs $1 to $150 per gallon. "So if you wanted to catch the city's entire runoff, the amount to comply with [EPA rules] would be $14 billion."

For that money, however, Frankel admits, "You'd also add another 9 percent to the city's water supply."

Cartoon by Ed Fischer. www.CartoonStock.com.

But to Frankel, that's not necessarily such a good thing. "Isn't that giving every developer in the city a water permit? The only thing stopping developers from going crazy is that Los Angeles doesn't have enough water to accommodate all their plans."

Reclaiming L.A. Wetlands Is Costly

"And in this case," Frankel continues, "river restoration pencils out to the most economical choice." It is expensive—he suspects it might be more than $15 billion. Daylighting streams and restoring wetlands would mean buying huge tracts of private property, ripping out its impervious surfaces and making sure those waterways have room to flood. "But once you've spent the money to acquire the land," Frankel points out, "it's self-maintaining. Unlike a treatment plant, it doesn't require power and tens of millions of dollars to maintain. If you're just worrying about your taxes, this is the best deal. Even the Coalition for Practical Regulation people, if they saw the viability of the river-restoration approach, they wouldn't oppose it. And think of all the parkland we'd create!"

Any way you do it, Frankel says, "We're facing the biggest public-works project in the history of the city. You're basically retrofitting a city that was developed in the wrong way. Los Angeles was not planned by visionaries. Back East, people knew they could neither pave over the streambeds, nor channelize streams; there was just too much water. Here, because the creeks were either dry or flooded so much of the year, we just said, 'Screw it. Let's get rid of them.'"

Frankel knows he's proposing a radical solution. "It's about changing the way we develop in a way that creates more parks and cleans up pollution," he says. "It's retrofitting the city in an environmentally sound way, as opposed to engineering in the old way.

EVALUATING THE AUTHOR'S ARGUMENTS:

This viewpoint outlines three options the city of Los Angeles could pursue to clean up urban runoff. Based on the information in the viewpoint, which option do you think would be the most successful, and why?

Viewpoint
7

Back-Pumping Is Necessary to Combat Drought Conditions

Sun-Sentinel

> *"Back-pumping has emerged as a necessary evil."*

Lake Okeechobee—one of the largest freshwater lakes in the United States—hit record-low levels on July 3, 2007. This southern Florida lake is the only source of drinking water for several adjacent towns and an important source of drinking water for West Palm Beach, Fort Meyers, and other large metropolitan areas. It is also the primary source of irrigation water for about half a million acres of sugar cane. In the following viewpoint the editors of the *Sun-Sentinel* argue that prolonged drought conditions make it necessary to back-pump water into Lake Okeechobee. Back-pumping would capture agricultural runoff water and pump it back into the lake, raising the water level but also raising the level of pollutants in the water.

AS YOU READ, CONSIDER THE FOLLOWING QUESTIONS:
1. According to this viewpoint, what is the advantage of back-pumping?
2. Why do the authors of this viewpoint describe the need for back-pumping as a "sad reality"?
3. According to this viewpoint, of what do the low levels of Lake Okeechobee remind Floridians?

Water management officials need to tread carefully in the debate over back-pumping water into Lake Okeechobee. The option presents a double-edged sword. It could secure drinking water and agriculture irrigation supplies, but at the risk of ushering pollutants into the lake. It is up for discussion today [August 8, 2007] during a South Florida Water Management District workshop because, despite the rains that have quenched thirsty lawns, Lake O's water levels are still dangerously below normal.

The advantage of back-pumping is it would add as much as a foot to water levels, which would provide a margin of error during the next dry season. Perhaps even more crucial, it could rescue the agri-

Prolonged severe drought conditions in Florida have caused Lake Okeechobee to drop five feet, leading some to suggest that back-pumping is needed to raise levels again.

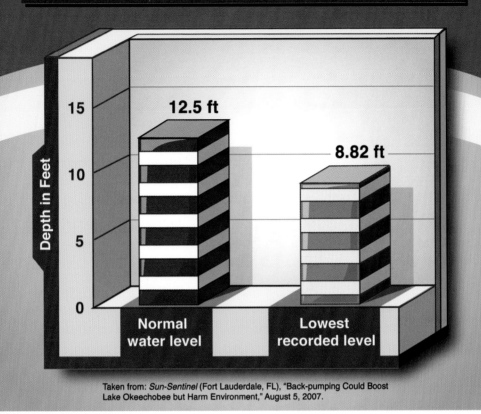

Lake Okeechobee Water Levels, July 3, 2007

12.5 ft

8.82 ft

Depth in Feet

15

10

5

0

Normal
water level

Lowest
recorded level

Taken from: *Sun-Sentinel* (Fort Lauderdale, FL), "Back-pumping Could Boost
Lake Okeechobee but Harm Environment," August 5, 2007.

cultural industry—one that helps feed Florida's economy—from the brink of potentially catastrophic crop losses next year if the drought indeed persists.

Drought Makes Back-Pumping Necessary

Water management officials believe drought conditions will continue once the rainy season ends, so the need to back-pump is almost a foregone conclusion.

The critical question is when to start. The unfortunate answer is soon.

> ## FAST FACT
>
> The Florida Farm Bureau considers back-pumping a tool that helps to balance the needs of agriculture, the environment, and municipalities.

With September approaching, we're deep into the rainy season, when atmospheric conditions make back-pumping more efficient.

Waiting much longer will remove back-pumping as a viable option, and we'll be left with no option at all to counteract a prolonged, crippling drought.

Back-Pumping Is a Sad Reality

It is a sad reality that this route must be taken after the district spent millions of dollars—wisely—to clean contaminated muck out of the lake floor after plummeting levels left it exposed. Back-pumping could erode those water-quality gains, even if it's by a relatively modest amount.

But because adequate water storage facilities were not built by the time this historic drought arrived, back-pumping has emerged as a necessary evil. It must, though, be looked upon as a temporary solution to a water-management crisis that only sufficient storage can effectively reverse in the long-term.

Florida Has a Water Crisis

The uncomfortable predicament should also serve as a reminder that water is not an infinite resource, and Floridians must become more conservation-minded, quickly. That makes year-round water restrictions even more essential, if for no other reason than to remind residents of their role in managing the crisis.

Bottom line: Sadly, it's a necessary evil at this point.

EVALUATING THE AUTHORS' ARGUMENTS:

According to this viewpoint, back-pumping water—contaminated with farmland fertilizers and pesticides—into Lake Okeechobee is not a first-choice strategy. The authors argue, however, that prolonged drought conditions make back-pumping necessary because people depend on the lake for drinking water and to irrigate crops. Do you feel the authors convincingly argue that filling the lake with polluted water is better than not filling the lake at all? Give reasons for your answers.

Back-Pumping Is Not Necessary

Andy Reid

"I can't vote for knowingly putting that much pollution into a water body [like Lake Okeechobee]."

The Everglades Agricultural Area (EAA)—about 700,000 acres—was designated by Congress to help feed the nation. Originally a wetland that lay one to five feet below water, this area was diked and drained to make it dry for farming. Crops grown on this land—mainly sugarcane—need to be irrigated. Water for irrigation comes from Lake Okeechobee. During the drought of 2006–2007, decreased rainfall meant an increased need for irrigation at a time when there was less water in Lake Okeechobee. To help mitigate the problem, agriculturalists wanted to back-pump runoff water back into the lake. Environmentalists opposed this because the runoff contains pollutants that would harm the lake. In the following viewpoint Andy Reid explains that, while back-pumping has been allowed in the past, on August 9, 2007, the South Florida Water Management District governing board voted against back-pumping because of environmental concerns. Andy Reid is a staff reporter for the *Sun-Sentinel*.

AS YOU READ, CONSIDER THE FOLLOWING QUESTIONS:
1. According to this viewpoint, what did agricultural representatives warn of?
2. With the lake at its lowest on record for that time of year, what did the district project, according to Andy Reid?
3. What does Reid report that phosphorus, nitrogen, and other nutrient-rich pollutants can lead to?

Rebuffing Big Sugar's water pleas, water managers on Thursday [August 9, 2007] refused to use Lake Okeechobee to store polluted stormwater that growers wanted to tap for drought-strained crops.

The South Florida Water Management District governing board decided environmental concerns outweighed the benefits of "back-pumping," which redirects water draining off agricultural land back into the lake to store for irrigation, also washing in fertilizers and other pollutants. Also, the board in a 4–3 vote rejected a compromise to pump in less-polluted water in smaller quantities than full-fledged back-pumping.

"I can't vote for knowingly putting that much pollution into a water body [like] the lake," governing board member Shannon Estenoz said.

Agricultural representatives warned of a looming economic "catastrophe" if the district didn't boost the lake level before the next dry season. "We can only pray that Mother Nature bails them out of their mistake," Judy Sanchez, spokeswoman for U.S. Sugar Corp., said about the vote. "It's obvious that some of the [board] members have been swayed by the extreme environmental groups that want to harm sugar farmers."

FAST FACT

Because of back-pumping of excessive fertilization, Lake Okeechobee now chronically suffers from toxic blue-green algae blooms. Blue-green algae toxins can affect the liver, nervous system, and skin. The toxins are not removed by chlorination, boiling, or algicides.

Better Options

As an alternative to back-pumping, the district agreed to explore storing water on more than 700 acres in Clewiston, old rock pits west of West Palm Beach and the 30,000-acre Holey Land and Rotenberger properties in southwestern Palm Beach County.

"We need a farm relief act of some kind to get them water," governing board Chairman Eric Buermann said. "Flush out the permitting and environmental concerns. . . . At least get that ball rolling."

The board also called for more long-term solutions, such as widening and deepening existing canals to store more water.

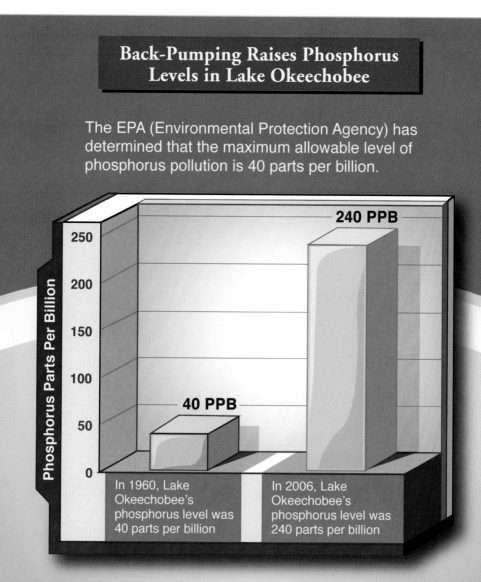

Back-Pumping Raises Phosphorus Levels in Lake Okeechobee

The EPA (Environmental Protection Agency) has determined that the maximum allowable level of phosphorus pollution is 40 parts per billion.

Phosphorus Parts Per Billion

240 PPB

40 PPB

In 1960, Lake Okeechobee's phosphorus level was 40 parts per billion

In 2006, Lake Okeechobee's phosphorus level was 240 parts per billion

Taken from: Lake Okeechobee Backpumping Fact Sheet, Earthjustice. http://www.earthjustice.org.

Agricultural runoff water in south Florida is cleaned and filtered at a pump station before it is pumped back into a water conservation area.

Agriculture faces an immediate crisis because of the drought and back-pumping provides the only immediate irrigation relief, said board member Malcolm Wade Jr., who works in the sugar industry. "This is a feel-good motion," Wade said about exploring the long-term possibilities.

Lake Level Reached a Record Low

On July 3, the lake dipped to its all-time low of 8.82 feet above sea level, and on Thursday it was up to only 9.48 feet. The district contends the lake needs to rise to at least 12.5 feet by November to be normal heading into the dry season.

With the lake at its lowest on record for this time of year, district projections anticipate water supply problems continuing into next year, raising the prospect of the first back-to-back years of water shortages since the 1980s. That would leave the lake, South Florida's primary backup water supply, with less water to replenish urban well fields, the Everglades and the irrigation canals tapped by agriculture.

The state projects economic impacts of a drought continuing into next year could hit $1 billion. "You are looking at crop failure in the Everglades Agricultural Area," Sanchez said.

Back-Pumping Does More Harm than Good

Back-pumping opponents argued that the amount of water saved would not be worth the environmental damage. "Back-pumping is in direct conflict with Everglades restoration," said Sara Fain, of the National Parks Conservation Association.

Phosphorus, nitrogen and other nutrient-rich pollutants that wash in with back-pumped water could lead to a "dead zone" in the lake, resulting from algae blooms and low oxygen levels that kill fish, insects and other parts of the lake's food chain.

Rejecting back-pumping signaled a stronger environmental focus for the district, coming from newly appointed members of the governing board.

EVALUATING THE AUTHORS' ARGUMENTS:

Both this and the preceding viewpoint reflect views that the drought will probably continue and the water level of Lake Okeechobee is dangerously low. However, the two viewpoints indicate disagreement on what is necessary to solve the problem. How do the ideas differ in these two viewpoints on where to store water for irrigation? Weighing both the agricultural needs of the area and the desire for a healthy lake, what do you feel is the best option for the areas deriving water from Lake Okeechobee? Cite examples.

Chapter 3

Who Can Solve the Water Management Problem?

A sign at a national park in Costa Rica reads, "Water Source . . . Throwing Garbage Prohibited . . . Keep This Area Clean . . . It Is the Water We All Consume."

The Global Community Needs to Unite to Solve the Water Problem

Alex Kirby and Vanessa Spedding

"[Global Water Partnership (GWP) is] a global organization that [promotes] dialogue on sector-spanning approaches to water management."

In the following viewpoint the Global Water Partnership (GWP) states that the amount of fresh water on Earth has remained constant. However, mankind's demands on this precious resource have changed. In recent decades, acceleration in human population and productivity have resulted in a world water crisis. To ensure enough water for everyone, GWP asserts that the global community needs to network, establish global policies, and make sure that all countries implement sustainable water resource management programs. To this end, GWP has sixty countries working together to develop integrated water resource management (IWRM). Alex Kirby and Vanessa Spedding are science writers based in the United Kingdom.

Alex Kirby and Venessa Spedding, *The Boldness of Small Steps: Ten Years of the Global Water Partnership*, Stockholm, Sweden: Global Water Partnership, 2006. Reproduced by permission.

AS YOU READ, CONSIDER THE FOLLOWING QUESTIONS:

1. According to this viewpoint, what is integrated water resource management (IWRM)?
2. Why were GWP partnerships created?
3. According to this viewpoint, between GWP's beginning in 1996 and 2006, how many regional and country partnerships formed?

I n the last decades of the 20th Century, the alarm signals about the state of the world's water were so clear that the international community had little choice but to sit up and take note. Participants at the United Nations Conference on Environment and Development, in Rio de Janeiro in June 1992, unveiled a sobering picture of global water resources: there was no doubt that they were in a critical state. The problems described were neither speculative in nature nor likely to affect our planet only in some distant future. The conference concluded with a call for action: political commitment was needed urgently at the highest levels of government, as indeed was change at the local level.

Preserving the precious and fragile resource that is our planet's water, which is of such enormous economic and social value, would require substantial investments, public awareness campaigns, legislative and institutional changes, technology development and capacity building programmes, beginning right away. The survival of many millions of people demanded immediate and effective action.

Fragmentation Equals Failure

But the conference also pinpointed a significant barrier to such action: the fragmentation of responsibility for the development and management of water resources between agencies in different sectors of the water arena. Unfortunately, degradation is moving faster than dialogue.

Building on the outcomes of the International Conference on Water and the Environment held just a few months previously in Dublin, Ireland (in January 1992)—namely the Dublin Statement and the Conference Report—as well as an analysis of earlier water conferences, the Rio conference called for mechanisms that would coordinate and promote the practice of integrated water resources management (IWRM). IWRM is a process that promotes the coordinated development and management of water, land and related resources in order to maximise the resultant economic and social welfare in an equitable manner without compromising the sustainability of vital ecosystems. IWRM puts in place specific, routine processes that ensure that different, water-using sectors work together on water services, water projects and water plans.

Everyone Must Get Involved
The Rio conference also emphasised the need to involve a broader range of people in water management policy and decision-making—in other words, not just the experts and officials. This would require greater

Professor Asit K. Biswas receives the Stockholm Water Prize from Crown Princess Victoria of Sweden for his work in solving global water resource problems.

Distribution of Earth's Water

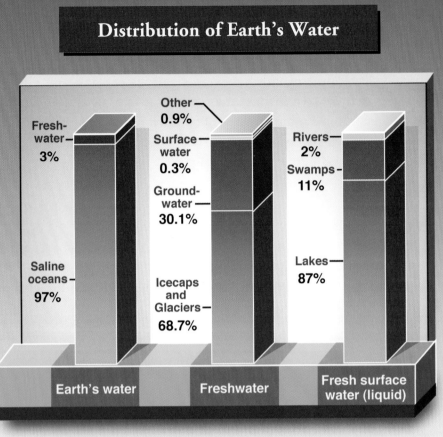

Taken from: U.S. Geological Survey (USGS). http://ga.water.usgs.gov/edu/waterdistribution.html.

public knowledge and participation, including by women, youth, indigenous people and local communities.

The stage was set for the creation of a new organisation. There were already many organizations with impressive expertise within specific water-related sectors, but none that could lead the way in integrating these areas of expertise. The new entity would need to get off the ground quickly and be light enough to operate with few resources. It would need the ability to mobilise the best minds and apply them to water management. It would have to be open enough to pull in, rather than alienate, the dozens of organisations already working in water. Ideally it would become a source of guidance on how to change existing investments in water resources while taking all needs into account. With luck, it would attract global attention to this emerging concept of a more integrated, more managed, more cherishing approach to water.

In 1996, the Global Water Partnership (GWP) was born. Its birth was made possible in practice by the coming together of the World Bank, the United Nations Development Programme (UNDP) and Sweden, which also offered to host the new organisation. These were quickly followed by other donors, including the UK and the Netherlands. The GWP was on its way.

International and Influential Leaders Are Important

As a new organisation, the GWP took a relatively new form: an active, purpose-built network of organisations combined with an international circle of influential water experts with the vision and influence to shape and steer the network. A small circle of donors was found who would both back the organisation and also engage actively with its work. A combination of 21st Century communication tools (email and the Internet), virtual organisational structures and an entrepreneurial spirit formed the glue to hold the framework together.

Now, ten years on, GWP information sources—particularly its publications—are used globally. Multi-stakeholder water partnerships have been established in 14 regions of the world and in more than 60 countries. There are almost 40 area partnerships (i.e. partnerships centred on and defined by a specific water catchment).

These GWP partnerships were created to start conversations between people who are from different sectors, organisations and traditions yet are united by a concern about how to develop, manage and share their increasingly scarce supplies of water. The partnerships try to be inclusive. Participants include government institutions, UN agencies, development banks, professional associations, academic bodies, non-governmental organisations (NGOs), private companies and community and other groups. In creating such a global, multi-stakeholder set-up, GWP filled a global gap in which now resides a network that is both different from

> **FAST FACT**
>
> According to UN secretary-general Ban Ki-Moon, 700 million people around the world are currently suffering from water scarcity, and that number could increase to more than 3 billion by 2025.

and complementary to the intergovernmental family of UN partnerships.

Partnerships Had Small Beginnings

Most regional and country GWP partnerships begin life as a small group of senior water experts who bring people together in their respective regions. Later, these groups—termed 'start engines' within GWP—transform into more formal, broad-based assemblies of stakeholders. These are called regional water partnerships and they are governed formally by representatives to ensure they are as inclusive and transparent as possible.

Since GWP's beginnings in 1996, a network of 14 regional partnerships and more than 60 country water partnerships has been formed in Central America; South America; the Caribbean; Southern, Eastern, Central and West Africa; the Mediterranean; Central and Eastern Europe; Central Asia and the Caucasus; South Asia; Southeast Asia; Australia; and China.

Help Countries Help Themselves

Each year, more country partnerships are established. Almost 10 area water partnerships have been created—working within countries at 'sub-national' level—in Central and Eastern Europe, Eastern Africa and South Asia.

The water partnerships are without doubt the operating arm of the GWP. It is these that help GWP to help others to help themselves. Strengthening the regional water partnerships and building country and sub-national water partnerships lie at the heart of the organisation.

This focus reflects a conscious effort by GWP to operate ever closer to the ground and to develop a dynamic, learning organisation, which promotes partnerships working close to the reality of water problems. This strategy does not, however, mean that the network as a whole is left to random organic growth: it is steered and coordinated by lean but strong administrative and governance systems.

GWP Became a Global Organization

The network had its first opportunity to meet under one roof four years into its existence, at the 2nd World Water Forum, held in the

Hague, the Netherlands, in March 2000. This was a landmark event for GWP, marking its establishment as a global organisation that promoted dialogue on sector-spanning approaches to water management. Prior to this meeting, each of the regional GWP partnerships had conducted a multi-stakeholder consultation process that resulted in the formulation of their own, regional strategies. These were published in their respective Vision to Action documents, and the key issues within then were fed into the Vision and *Framework for Action* documents published by the World Water Council and GWP for discussion at the forum.

As a map for realising the goals in the Vision, GWP produced a document entitled: *Towards Water Security: A Framework for Action.* This set out new perspectives on how things could be changed—by moving away from fragmented approaches and towards an integrated solution to common water problems. A further small step in the right direction had been taken.

EVALUATING THE AUTHORS' ARGUMENTS:

In this viewpoint the authors explain that the goal of Global Watership Partnership is to help less-developed countries implement sustainable water resource management. As differing sectors of a country vie for increased use of water for irrigation, sewage, energy, transportation, recreation, or drinking water, why is it important for the various sectors to cooperate, and how can countries benefit from a global perspective, and global support? Give reasons for your answer.

Government Needs to Solve the Water Problem

"If a country lacks essential freedoms, like the freedom of speech and the right to organize, promoting participatory approaches in water development programmes is compromised."

Gordon Young, Carlos Fernandez-Jauregui, et al.

In the following viewpoint, taken from the United Nations Educational, Scientific and Cultural Organization (UNESCO) 2006 water report, the authors assert that poor government policy is often at the root of a country's water problems. Governments that instigate, tolerate, or perpetuate armed conflicts historically add to the world's water problems, as wars destroy vital water infrastructures. Stable governments, on the other hand, can do much to improve a country's water policies. In the early 1990s South Africa's water problem was solved not by finding more water but by creating a democratic government that was willing to redistribute water resources to benefit poor people. Democratic governments, however, can also contribute to water problems when they engage in patronage politics. Such a circumstance occurs when governments

Gordon Young, Carlos Fernandez-Jauregui, et. al., *Water: A Shared Responsibility: The United Nations World Water Development Report 2,* Danvers, MA: United Nations Educational, Scientific and Cultural Organization (UNESCO) and Berghahn Books, 2006. © UNESCO-WWAP 2006. All rights reserved. Used with permission of UNESCO, and by Berghahn Books, conveyed through Copyright Clearance Center, Inc.

allow groups to exploit water by circumventing environmental regulations in exchange for giving financial support to a particular political party or candidate.

AS YOU READ, CONSIDER THE FOLLOWING QUESTIONS:
1. According to this viewpoint, what effects do wars and social and political unrest have on people and water resources?
2. According to this viewpoint, what water challenges are faced by an estimated twenty-six countries with a combined population of more than 350 million people?
3. According to this viewpoint, democratization without the appropriate checks and balances can lead to what water management problems?

T he past decades have witnessed tremendous social, political and economic changes. The end of the cold war and the process of decolonization continue to shape current societal events. Globalization and the increasing speed of information exchange have had tremendous impacts on societies. Terrorism has also had a major impact on how countries interact with each other and on how governments interact with their citizens. Some commentators worry that we are heading towards a more closed 'barbed-wire' society in an effort to keep out threats, while others feel that our new means of communication and economic growth make for more open societies.

The way we perceive and govern our water resources is also rooted in culture. But although water is considered by most cultures to be something critical for all life, with a prominent place in cultural and religious beliefs, it is something of a paradox that water is often taken for granted and is increasingly polluted, with many people having limited access to clean drinking water and water for productive activities.

Governments Can Delegate Water Management
The development of governance and management systems within the water sector is closely related to overall development trends in which the role of the state has shifted from the provider to the enabler of development and welfare [the 'rolling back of the state']. By 2000,

national, provincial and local governments in ninety-three countries had begun to privatize drinking water and wastewater services. Between 1995 and 1999, governments around the world privatized an average of thirty-six water supply or wastewater treatment systems annually. Despite the push for increased privatization, the water-services sector remains one of the last public 'bastions'. Water still remains an area that is generally heavily dependent on public investment and regulations in developed and developing countries alike.

Wars Compound the Water Problem

War and social and political unrest demolish people's lives and livelihood, as well as destroy important water resources, disrupting water services and impacting negatively on governance. Between 1990 and 2000, 118 armed conflicts worldwide claimed approximately 6 million lives. War will have long-term effects and will continue to affect people's livelihood, opportunities and access to natural resources and public services many years after the actual conflict has ended. In 2001 it was estimated that some 12 million refugees and 5 million 'internally displaced persons' were forced to settle in resource-scarce areas, putting further pressure on people, water and the environment. Recent conflicts in Kosovo, Afghanistan and Iraq have led to the destruction of economically vital water infrastructures, and many people are deprived of safe drinking water and basic sanitation as well as sufficient water for productive uses.

The resolution of conflict and social and political instability can sometimes yield unexpected opportunities for fundamental changes in society that can lead to improved policy-making, which in turn can benefit a nation's water prospects. The political changes in South Africa in the early 1990s and the emergence of a democratic system have allowed for reform of the water sector in the areas of policy, organizational structure, water rights and legislation. South African water reform is a very comprehensive and innovative approach to water management, allowing for more holistic, people-centred and ecological approaches to the governance of water. It also aims at redistributing water resources to the benefit of poor people.

Many Factors Affect Governmental Decisions

Democratization, macroeconomic changes, population growth and other demographic changes, and social and political instability often

Democratic Policies Are Among Several Factors Necessary for Successful Water Governance

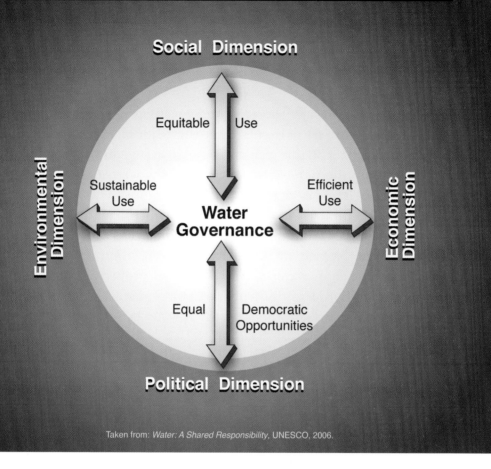

Taken from: *Water: A Shared Responsibility*, UNESCO, 2006.

have much greater impacts on water use and demands than any water policy itself. Global market conditions and trade regimes are factors that affect crop choices and thus also have serious implications for water use and demands in agriculture. Market liberalization can contribute to improving the water situation for many people but can also increase pressures to overexploit water and the environment. . . .

Improved Governance and Water Shortages Present Double Challenge

Increasing water demands will lead to a decline of per capita supply in the future. Currently, an estimated twenty-six countries with a combined population of more than 350 million people are located in regions with severe water scarcity where the available water resources seem to be sufficient to meet reasonable water needs for development activities, *but* only if these countries take appropriate water demand and supply management measures. In many countries, there will also be additional, sometimes severe, local water scarcities, even within countries that have sufficient aggregate water resources, such as within the US and India.

A comparison of water shortages and governance challenges shows that many countries, particularly in the Middle East and North Africa, are facing a double challenge. It is also evident that countries that have bountiful water resources are facing governance challenges to provide water and sanitation services *and* protect water resources. For example, countries in Central Africa, which have ample water resources, have not been able to provide their citizens with a sufficient supply of water, hence the point that water provision is often less a question of available water resources than of properly functioning institutions and proper infrastructure management. Despite limited democratic provisions in some countries, water can still be managed in more democratic ways at the local level, such as through water-user associations or other types of local organizations.

Democracy Is Not the Entire Solution

It has been suggested that partial democratization, without the appropriate checks and balances, can, at least in the short run, lead to an increase in the exploitation of water, land and forests through patronage politics. It has also been suggested that within well-established democratic polities, politicians can make environmental 'pay-offs' to groups that financially support the campaigns of a particular party or candidate. These 'pay-offs' can include, for example, circumventing certain environmental regulations and allowing the lax enforcement of pollution control. Despite the fact that democracy has flourished in Western Europe, more than half of European cities are currently exploiting groundwater at unsustainable rates. Chronic water shortages already affect 4.5 million people in Catalonia, where authorities are pressing for the construction of a pipeline to divert water from the Rhone in France to Barcelona. It is thus apparent that many water development 'principles'—IWRM [Integrated Water Resources

Management] participation, transparency, community involvement and decentralization—require improved governance in order to be successfully implemented. It is unlikely that effective participation and transparency within the water sector will take place unless there are overall changes in how societies and political systems function.

Political Rights and Civil Liberties Can Vary

Water policy reform, IWRM implementation and meeting the Millennium Development Goals (MDGs) all require that we address issues in the water and development interface, as well as issues that have traditionally been considered outside the scope of water. If we wish to increase stakeholder participation, make decentralization more effective and hold water agencies and utilities accountable, enhanced democratization is required. Yet fairly little is known about the local and practical links between water shortages and democratization. The general notion is that democratization is beneficial to improved water governance and would open up for more transparency, decentralization and participation. But in which ways? How big an impact would it make? And what type of democratization makes the biggest impact? The cases of India (low levels of water services) and southern Spain (dwindling groundwater) indicate that democracy itself is not sufficient. It also depends on how political rights and civil liberties are exercised, as well as on other factors, such as demographic development, economic growth, institutional effectiveness and how welfare is generated and distributed within and between societies. This does not mean that water managers should refrain from trying to make

FAST FACT

Bill Richardson, governor of New Mexico, believes government should play a role in water issues: "I want a national water policy. We need a dialogue between states to deal with issues like water conservation, water reuse technology, water delivery and water production."

a difference, but rather underlines an urgent need to collaborate with new actors outside the water realm and establish more inclusive water development networks. Political change has to begin somewhere, and in

Rebels in Colombia frequently target the energy grid, water reservoirs, and oil pipelines, making it difficult for people to have stable access to water resources.

some cases the promotion of improved water governance may even serve as an avant-garde for inducing broad-based reform. It has been pointed out that cooperative water development in the Netherlands in the earlier part of the twentieth century was an important part of nation-building for the modern Dutch welfare state.

Citizens Must Be Able to Hold Government Agencies Accountable

Improved governance and impacts on water resources management and related services are both complex and dynamic. If a country lacks essential freedoms, like the freedom of speech and the right to organize, promoting participatory approaches in water development programmes is compromised. If citizens cannot access basic information on water quantity and quality, it seriously curtails their chances of halting environmentally unsound water projects or to hold relevant government agencies accountable.

EVALUATING THE AUTHORS' ARGUMENTS:

According to this viewpoint, countries with democratic governments traditionally have more equitable water policies than countries with other types of governments. And yet, democracy too has its pitfalls. Even in countries with mature democracies, such as the United States, citizens sometimes take water for granted and waste millions of gallons of household water every day. In addition, water can be polluted when "patronage politics" induces government officials to compromise enforcement of environmental regulations for groups who give large financial contributions to a particular political party or candidate. In your opinion, which of these two problems do you feel does the most harm to water resource management in the United States? What democratic methods (freedom of speech, freedom to organize, public elections, and the like) do you think would be most effective in solving the problem?

Corporate Investment Is Needed to Solve the Water Problem

IFAT CHINA

"According to analysts' estimates, the market for water treatment in China is growing at a rate of 15 percent per year."

According to the following viewpoint, China is experiencing a severe and protracted water crisis. Over 300 million people are without access to clean drinking water, 90 percent of the surface water is seriously polluted, and over 60 percent of all Chinese cities lack sewage systems. Projected increases in population and economic expansion will add to an already difficult problem. The authors explain that the government of China has neither the money nor the expertise to solve its problem, and China welcomes the investments of Western businesses and technology firms. Already, private water companies are managing the water supplies in several large cities in China. In 2008 China will host the third IFAT CHINA environmental trade fair, which invites business and technology leaders to display water products and solutions and gives companies the opportunity to initiate new business contracts in China.

"IFAT CHINA 2008: Water Is Big Business," IFAT CHINA Press Release, June 26, 2007. Reproduced by permission.

The environmental problems facing China arising from the country's economic expansion and rapid urbanisation are leading to a surge in demand for water and waste-water treatment technology. The environmental trade fair IFAT CHINA, which takes place from 23 to 25 September 2008 in Shanghai gives international technology suppliers the opportunity to present their services and products in this growth market.

In the Chinese cities, 90 percent of the surface water and 50 percent of the ground water is seriously polluted. According to information from the German Chambers of Commerce Abroad, only 20 to 25 percent of the waste water occurring nationwide is treated. Over 60 percent of all Chinese cities have no sewage systems. Other figures underline the critical situation in the supply of water in China. China's State Environmental Protection Administration (SEPA) quotes a figure of over 300 million people in China who have no access to clean drinking water. 90 percent of the rivers and 75 percent of the lakes in the country are polluted or seriously polluted.

This water pollution is leading to economic losses for China, not to mention the impact on the country's ecology and the health of its population. The Chinese Academy of Science estimates that in 2003 the losses through water and air pollution accounted for 15 percent of the national product.

China Has Set High Goals

Against this background—and not least because of the intensified national and international debate about the environment—the Chinese government has set itself high goals in its 11th Five-Year Plan (2006 to 2010) regarding waste water. By 2010 at least 70 percent

In an effort to provide safer drinking water, control pollution, and increase water conservation, China is encouraging Western businesses to invest and initiate new contracts in China.

of all sewage in towns will be treated. For the cities of Beijing and Shanghai the goals are even more ambitious—Beijing must increase the proportion of sewage treated from 50 percent at present levels to 90 percent by the Olympic Games in 2008. In Shanghai a treatment rate of 80 percent is to be reached by Expo 2010. In general all cities with over 250,000 inhabitants will be equipped with sewage plants.

Existing sewage-treatment plants are to be modernised. For this 32 billion euros' worth of investment is envisaged.

According to analysts' estimates, the market for water treatment in China is growing at a rate of 15 percent per year. Many foreign firms have been benefiting from this development for several years. The French water giant Suez is already present in a number of Chinese cities. In the industrial zone in Shanghai Suez has set up a sewage-treatment plant and taken a 60 percent stake in a water project in the southwestern Chinese city of Chongqing. At the beginning of 2006 Suez moved into its regional headquarters in Shanghai and in July last year it set up a research institute in Shanghai.

Western Water Companies Supply Many Services

Another French water group, Veolia water, signed its 21st contract for water-supply services in China in January this year. This new project covers a range of services, including, from mid 2007, the operation of four water-treatment plants in Lanzhou, the capital of Gansu province, with a total capacity of 2.2 million cubic metres per year.

FAST FACT

Inventor Dean Cameron was awarded the Global Award at the 2005 World Expo for creating Biolytix—a sewage treatment system deemed "an environmental technology that has the potential to solve global environmental problems." This chemical-free system uses worms and other organisms to convert waste into irrigation water.

One example of German-Chinese involvement comes from the Berlinwasser Group, which has built a sewage plant in Nanchang, the capital of Jiangxi Province in the southwest of China. This plant treats sewage for around one million inhabitants.

In industrial waste-water treatment, too, foreign expertise is in demand. For example, the Industrial Solutions and Services division of Siemens recently designed and built a treatment plant for removing nitrogen from waste water for the pharmaceuticals company Degussa Rexim (Nanning) Pharmaceutical Co. in the southern Chinese town of Wuming. This plant, based on biochemical treatment technology, has an annual capacity of around 300,000 cubic metres of water.

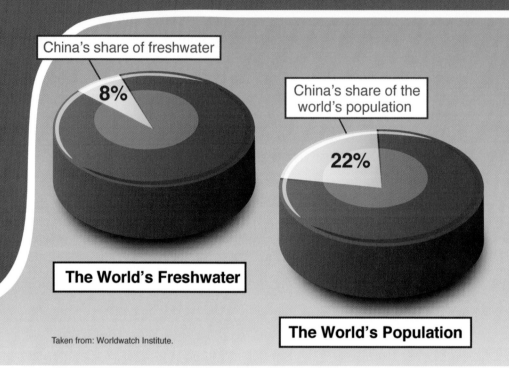

China Has a Water Problem

China's share of freshwater

8%

The World's Freshwater

China's share of the world's population

22%

The World's Population

Taken from: Worldwatch Institute.

Western Companies Bring in Experts and Technology

"The Peoples Republic of China is one of the most important pillars in our business in the Asian-Pacific region, and it is becoming ever more important in our global operations," said Prof. Dr. Hermann Requardt, a member of the board of Siemens AG at the inauguration of the 'Siemens Corporate Technology China' research centre at the end of October last year in Beijing. Over 300 scientists will be carrying out research here into new environmental, energy, health and automation technologies. Siemens will be investing around 80 million euros per year in the location up to 2010.

In line with the importance of the subject of water in China, sewage treatment and drinking water preparation will again be major focuses at the environmental trade fair IFAT CHINA in September 2008 in Shanghai. Already at the last event in June 2006, there was a strong presence among the exhibitors from companies offering products and system solutions for water and waste-water treatment. But also for the fields of refuse handling, recycling, measurement technology, air-pollution control and renewable energies, IFAT CHINA is regarded as an important international networking platform—at IFAT CHINA 2006, 284 exhibitors from 25 countries successfully initiated new business and forged valuable new contacts in China.

EVALUATING THE AUTHORS' ARGUMENTS:

According to this viewpoint, "water pollution is leading to economic losses for China." To solve this problem, China is outsourcing its water management to private water companies from Western nations. In your opinion, aside from giving people clean water, what other benefits might arise from bringing Western companies to China?

Women Are Needed to Solve the Water Problem

Julie Fisher

"*Women can and do make a contribution to water and sanitation services and do have a right as human beings to participate in issues that affect their lives and those of their families.*"

According to the Water Supply and Sanitation Collaborative Council (WSSCC), there are still 2.6 billion people worldwide without access to sanitation facilities and 1.1 billion people without access to safe drinking water. These people live in poor, overcrowded, or developing areas of the world and typically it is up to the women and girls to provide water and ensure hygiene for the family. In the following viewpoint, the WSSCC, which helps communities acquire water and sanitation facilities, asserts that since women are at the center of water issues, they are also in the best position to identify and manage sustainable solutions. The WSSCC was mandated by the United Nations to serve people around the world who lack water and sanitation. The Water, Engineering, and Development Centre (WEDC) is one of the world's leading institutions devoted to improving the health of people in need. Julie Fisher is a researcher and writer for WEDC; she has authored numerous scientific reports on water management.

Julie Fisher, "For Her It's the Big Issue: Putting Women at the Centre of Water Supply, Sanitation, and Hygiene," Geneva, Switzerland: Water Supply and Sanitation Collaborative Council, 2006. Reproduced by permission.

AS YOU READ, CONSIDER THE FOLLOWING QUESTIONS:
  1. According to this viewpoint, what did a World Bank evaluation of 122 water projects find?
  2. What did the United Nations (UN) Interagency Task Force on Gender and Water find out about women managers?
  3. According to this viewpoint, what changes in water-related diseases does the author say took place following the implementation of water supply projects?

I t is estimated that women and girls in low-income countries spend 40 billion hours every year fetching and carrying water from sources which are often far away and may not, after all, provide clean water.

From this standpoint, it is simple to understand that a woman could be empowered by having a nearby pump that conveniently supplies enough safe water to her family. Easier access to such basic services enables women to identify and grasp new opportunities for themselves, to grow in confidence and attain a greater sense of personal dignity. . . .

Women Play an Important Role

There is evidence to show that water and sanitation services are generally more effective if women take an active role in the various stages involved in setting them up, from design and planning, through to the ongoing operations and maintenance procedures required to make any initiative sustainable. As well as dealing with these technical and practical issues, women have an important role in educating their families and the community about hygienic practices. Again, evidence suggests that their involvement makes these ventures more likely to succeed.

The effects of both improved service provision and better knowledge about hygiene are felt throughout the wider community, most obviously through improved general health and quality of life. There are more subtle effects of these measures on the lives of women, such as greater confidence, increased capacity to earn money, and the fact that women are likely to be healthier, happier and have more time to concentrate on making the home a better place in which to live. Again, ultimately, what is good for women is good for the family and the whole community, who share the benefit from all these improvements.

Some Oppose Leadership by Women

There is sometimes opposition to positioning women at the centre of water resource management initiatives, even when this comes as a response to a directive to include a majority or quota of women in decision-making. This opposition is usually because women are seen to be stepping outside their traditional, non-public roles into public and technical areas for which they are perceived to be unqualified and unsuited. However, women can and do make a contribution to water and sanitation services and do have a right as human beings to participate in issues that affect their lives and those of their families. Women bear the main responsibility for keeping their households supplied with water, caring for the sick, maintaining a hygienic domestic environment and bringing up healthy children. It is they who are most likely to know what is required and where. Getting these important details right means better services and quality of life for all in the community.

A World Bank evaluation of 122 water projects found that the effectiveness of a project was six to seven times higher where women were involved than where they were not. The examples given here demonstrate this in many different locations and in various ways.

Women Need to Be Involved from the Start

The results of involving women in the design and planning stages are multiple, from reducing corruption, increasing management transparency, better financial management and empowering women by example.

In Indonesia and Malawi, women overcame deeply entrenched prejudices about their lack of technical understanding, showing that, as primary users of water, they were the most qualified to comment on an appropriate design for a water system. What is seen to be new territory for women was quickly scaled up in Indonesia and the benefits extended to others.

Women Identified Design Errors The women of the Sewukan community in the Magelan district of Java, Indonesia, took part in a consultation on community water systems. In spite of a degree of prejudice about women's lack of technical knowledge, they identified useful technical alterations to existing design errors, which were the basis of modifications to the new water system. Further improvements were made in the form of more equitable distribution of water supply and the addition of a sanitation facility. Prior to taking part in the consultation process, women in the community had not been accustomed to publicly discussing issues other than those relating to social and religious topics. Their input into this project resulted in the establishment of more community committees in other neighbourhoods,

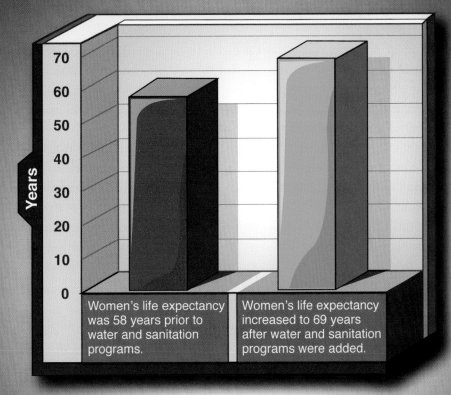

Water Is a Matter of Life and Death

A 2003 study indicated that in Malaysia, when the government added water and sanitation programs to health care, women began living nearly 20% longer.

Years

70
60
50
40
30
20
10
0

Women's life expectancy was 58 years prior to water and sanitation programs.

Women's life expectancy increased to 69 years after water and sanitation programs were added.

Taken from: Julie Fisher, "For Her It's the Big Issue," WSSCC and WEDC, March 2006.

which participated in project design and in monitoring the quality of construction. . . .

Women Know How to Find Water In the Kilombero district of Tanzania, a water well which was built by an NGO dried up shortly after it was created. When development workers talked to the local women, they reported that the location of the well had been decided on by a local committee consisting only of men, and that they had made their decision only on the basis of geographical criteria. Women, on the other hand, demanded that the soil conditions also be taken into account. Where water is scarce in Tanzania, it is often the task of women to dig for it by hand, and consequently, they know the places which provide the best water yields. Since that incident, women in the Kilombero district have had more involvement in decisions about where water wells should be dug.

Women Took Political Action Women in the Ukraine exerted effective pressure on powerful authorities to bring about change to unsafe and unfair practices. The town of Luzanivka in the Ukraine experienced problems caused by an inadequate sewage system that would result in an overflow of sewage onto the streets. MAMA-86 is an environmental women's organisation that was formed after the Chernobyl disaster [a massive nuclear accident in Ukraine, 1986]. In 2000, it launched a political campaign, filing a law suit against the authority responsible. The result was that the government funded the construction of a sewage pump and closed the oil-tank cleaning facility from which the problems were originating. MAMA-86's other achievements have included water main repairs, installation of water meters to reduce very high water bills, plus reimbursements to those who had overpaid.

Women Use Money Wisely

According to the UN [United Nations] Interagency Task Force on Gender and Water, women have been found to be the most effective managers in several UN water projects in Africa, where water has been used for income generation and where women have control over income earned from their small-scale enterprises. Women's cooperatives connected to water points in Mauritania, for example, have become very dynamic and women take a more active and prominent role through capacity building and provision of credit. For example, women in Lesotho have a tradition of saving small amounts of money each month for important purposes. Such traditional sources of investment can be used for water and sanitation facilities if supplemented by seed money from NGOs or other sources.

There are many other instances of women successfully taking responsibility for generating or administering funding for WASH [water, sanitation, and hygiene] improvements.

In many parts of the developing world women and girls are responsible for collecting the water their families use for drinking, cooking, and cleaning.

In Keelakarthigaipatti, India, a Water Partners International project, the Sustainable Health through Water and Sanitation Program (2004) has brought about significant improvements in the water supply and sanitation facilities. A central role has been played by a Women's Self-Help group, which is in charge of the loan fund within the community. Women involved with this have enjoyed the additional benefits of their new leadership roles, with responsibility for funding the project, construction of facilities and the project's successful completion. . . .

Women Raise Public Awareness

A key component of any WASH project is to raise awareness about the importance of carrying out safe hygienic practices. Women play a vital role in awareness-raising about these issues, as they take the main responsibility for domestic duties and for developing safe and hygienic habits in children. Women also cope with the additional burden of caring for household members who become sick as a result of unsafe water and poor sanitation. . . .

A striking example of public awareness efforts that encouraged women's participation is the Journalist Orientation Programmes which were organised by the Nepal WASH Group in three regions before launching a media campaign in March 2004 to coincide with National Sanitation Week. The objective was to make the media realise that sanitation was one of the big issues impacting on people's lives. Particularly encouraging was the response from women journalists, a significant achievement considering that the media is dominated by males in Nepal.

Established in 2002, the "WASH Media Award" encourages journalists in developing countries to provide better coverage of WASH issues to raise public awareness. At the 2004 Global WASH Forum in Senegal, the first recipient of the award was Ms. Nadia El-Awady, an Egyptian science reporter for "Islam Online." The Nile and Its People described the impacts of industrial pollution, sewage and solid waste management on people's health and dignity along the River Nile and was broadcast as a TV documentary on BBC World. . . .

More Water Means Better Health

Following the implementation of water supply projects, the incidence of water-related diseases decreased, according to WaterAid's studies of water provision in Ethiopia, Ghana, India and Tanzania. Projects in India reduced the incidence of scabies, diarrhoeal episodes and child mortality. Also in Atwedie, Ghana, bilharzia, scabies and yaws have been eradicated from the village.

Coupled with improvements in hygiene practice, this leads to better general health for the whole community. For example, households with a 10 per cent increase in water use for cleaning purposes enjoyed a 1.3% decrease in the occurrence of diarrhoea. Having convenient amenities and plenty of water on tap also enables women to maintain more hygienic standards of childcare. It was found that the existence of a yard tap nearly doubled the odds of a mother washing her hands after cleaning a child's anus, and doubled the chances of her washing faecally-soiled linen immediately.

Women have the best local knowledge about common habits and any problems stemming from them. They are therefore central to educating their families and other community members about the benefits of using safe water, adequate sanitation and practising good hygiene, as the following examples show:

Winnie Miyando Cheolo and Febby Temb Mwachingwala are members of a women's group in Mwachingwala village, Zambia, which has actively promoted sanitation and hygiene issues since 1998. During this time, they have been involved in building latrines for every household. Other hygiene initiatives carried out have been the promotion of the use of dish racks, rubbish pits and washing facilities, all of which have impacted to reduce the incidence of disease in the village. Another important improvement is that children are taught about good hygiene practice.

The Clearwater Project is being implemented in the Gualcinse community in Honduras. Gladis Maribel Dias is one of its beneficiaries as she now has piped water and a "pila" (outdoor wash basin). She states that she was motivated to have a water supply in her home because it guarantees her family a better life. Each household is offered a latrine and a bath, which provide residents with the opportunity to enjoy a level of hygiene and personal cleanliness as well as the benefits of basic sanitation.

Group initiatives with women in the community have proven to be an effective way of transmitting key WASH messages, which bring about radical changes in the health of the community.

EVALUATING THE AUTHOR'S ARGUMENTS:

According to this viewpoint, water and sanitation projects designed to help communities in poor and developing nations are most likely to succeed if local women are directly involved in the planning, implementing, and long-term management of the projects. In contrast, in the United States, successful water and sewer projects are not dependent on management by women. In your opinion, why does this difference exist? Cite examples and findings from this viewpoint in your answer.

Teenagers Are Needed to Solve the Water Problem

"Youths . . . 'take their messages to their schools, their families and friends. . . . They create a domino effect.'"

Monica Campbell

In the following viewpoint Monica Campbell explains that in 2006, 100 youths from 30 countries participated in the Children's Water Forum in Mexico City. Simultaneously, 11,000 adults from 100 countries participated in the 4th World Water Forum. Campbell notes that the teens focused on cooperative action, homegrown solutions, and personal involvement. In contrast, the adult-led seminars focused on ideological feuds, politics, and corporate agendas. Campbell, a journalist based in Mexico City, regularly contributes to the *Christian Science Monitor*.

AS YOU READ, CONSIDER THE FOLLOWING QUESTIONS:
1. According to this viewpoint, what water policies are promoted at the adult-led seminars in Mexico City?
2. What challenges does Ethopian Ojulu Okelli face in his town of Gambella, according to Monica Campbell?
3. In this viewpoint, what does Claire Hajaj, a UNICEF spokeswoman, say about youths?

Monica Campbell, "As Experts Ponder World Water Crisis, Teenagers Show Creativity," *The Christian Science Monitor,* March 22, 2006, p. 1. Copyright © 2006 The Christian Science Publishing Society. Reproduced by permission of the author.

As water experts meet in Mexico City to debate the world's daunting water crisis, 15-year-old Dolly Akhter is here to share her simple approach. She and 6,000 other girls canvass the slums of Dhaka, going door to door in the Bangladeshi capital to tout good hygiene. "We talk to families and especially the teenage girls about the importance of washing their hands," explains Dolly.

She is among 100 or so children from more than 30 countries participating in the Children's Water Forum held parallel to the 4th World Water Forum. While the adults argue over ideological differences, the youngsters showcase the grass-roots action that reaches those hardest hit by the lack of safe water and basic sanitation:

Teenagers Lead the Way
- Suresh Baral, 13, leads a club in rural Nepal that helps communities pay for toilets through microfinancing;
- As leader of Nigeria's Children Parliament, 15-year-old Ibrahim Adamuy implores government officials to put aside their "mounds of paper" and talk about solutions;
- Anyeli González, 16, heads a program at her high school in Colombia that brings in local storytellers, puppeteers, and water company executives to raise environmental awareness;
- 9th-grader Happy Sisomphone directs a radio program in Laos to improve sanitation.

"Youth-led ideas may seem simple," says Jamal Shagir, the World Bank's director of water and energy. "But they represent fantastic opportunities for changing behavior and attitudes within communities. The international community must continue to push these programs along and harness young people's energy."

Teens Meet with Adults
In the conference halls, the teenagers mix with the larger forum's 11,000 adult participants—industry leaders, government ministers, and nongovernmental groups—from more than 100 countries.

Adult-led seminars on water policy have been marked by ideological feuds: Business-friendly politicians and corporations promote privatization and private sector control over water delivery, while others—who also push their agenda in street protests outside the conference—believe water is a public domain that should be managed by communities.

Just like the older experts here, the teenage activists rattle off the grim facts: More than a billion people are without adequate sewage and sanitation, according to the United Nations (UN), and more than 3 million deaths a year are blamed on water-borne disease.

Teens Focus on Cooperation

The teenagers tend to avoid politics and corporate agendas and focus on cooperative action. They're here to learn about each other's projects and spread the word to more children. "We must all fight together to change our lives and those of others," says Dolly, who was flown here from her bamboo-and-tin home by the United Nations Children's Fund (UNICEF). "How can we stand by and let children die if there are solutions?"

Children from thirty countries in the Children's Water Forum read a statement during the 4th World Water Forum in Mexico City in 2006.

Vanessa Tobin, chief of UNICEF's water and sanitation section, appreciates the straightforward talk. "There's no diplomacy in their dialogue. It's all very direct and very honest."

Ms. Tobin's section also runs education programs at schools in more than 70 countries, and helped kick-start Dhaka's hygiene education program. Such youth-led projects are often launched and funded by UNICEF and other groups, such as the US-based nonprofit Water Education for Teachers and the humanitarian agency Oxfam. They hope that getting kids involved at the grass-roots level now will pay off in the long term.

"When you get young people involved at an early enough age, you're putting in place a mind-set that will be there 20 years from now," says Tobin. "The experiences these children are having now won't be forgotten."

Teens Overcome Obstacles

Suresh's toilet-financing project in Nepal, started with advice from UNICEF, is already producing results: Two-thirds of homes in his village of Pumbi Bhumbi now have toilets, he says. "Bit by bit, we're managing to bring change," he affirms.

Ethiopian Ojulu Okelli hopes to get running water and latrines in his school, but few places pose a bigger challenge for water activists than his town of Gambella on the border with southern Sudan. It's an area mired in absolute poverty that is just now recovering from years of ethnic conflict. Okelli only gets access to clean water when his mother and sister return from their five-kilometer walk from the nearest well.

> **FAST FACT**
>
> Around 5,760 children die each day (4 per minute, 2.1 million each year) from illnesses associated with a lack of drinking water, basic sanitation, and poor hygiene—the equivalent of thirty Boeing 747s, filled with children, crashing each day.

Ojulu and his friends spotted a chance to improve their underdog surroundings by getting involved in their school's environmental club. "We started cleaning up the grounds on Saturdays, picking up the litter and all that," he says, adding that he hopes that community

The United States Has Millions of Teens Who Could Help Solve the Water Problem

267,000,000
General population
of United States
(not including
teens)

33,000,000
12–19-year-olds

Compiled by editor

leaders will notice the cleanups and bring tap water and latrines to the school.

"The girls need this especially," adds Okelli, who is aware that menstruation means an inconvenient and humiliating trip to a lone bush— sometimes causing girls to drop out of school when they hit puberty.

In other parts of Africa, schoolkids spin on brightly colored merry-go-rounds that pump water from nearby wells when spun. About 600 UNICEF-financed "play pumps" are now in place in South Africa.

Meanwhile, in his southeastern village in Laos, spiky-haired Happy Sisomphone directs a radio segment on sanitation, hygiene, and waterborne diseases. "In school we're reminded that it's important to wash your hands after playing with dirt," says Happy, trained by UNICEF as a volunteer radio producer. "But we never learn why. So I interview people about the reasons we should be careful."

UNICEF Supports Teens' Projects

Claire Hajaj, a UNICEF spokeswoman, considers youths "incomparably useful" to community projects. "They take their messages to their schools, their families and friends," she says. "They create a domino effect. And if adults see kids leading these initiatives then they think, oh, I can do this, too."

Already, a good deal of the talk at the forum has centered on local, homegrown solutions. At the same time, UN studies highlighted that bringing such solutions requires tighter cooperation between governments and private companies, with less of an eye on profits.

But despite the good intentions, some of the youths run into walls. When Happy started up his radio show, some villagers rejected the idea of a young voice over the radio waves lecturing about the ills generated by bad water. "Big messages from little people don't always work," he says. "But little by little people tend to come around."

EVALUATING THE AUTHOR'S ARGUMENTS:

According to this viewpoint, the teenage participants did not have the money or the power possessed by the corporate and governmental leaders who attended the water forum, and yet the youths were clearly making a difference in their communities. In your opinion, what assets do these teens possess, and how do they use their assets to help solve the water problem? Cite examples in your explanation.

Facts About Water Resource Management

Basic Water Usage and Availability

- The average water usage per person per day in the United States is 100 gallons.
- Showering (wet down, soap up, and rinse off) uses approximately 4 gallons of water. Filling a bathtub uses approximately 10 to 12 gallons.
- Brushing teeth (wet brush and rinsing briefly) uses approximately half a gallon of water.
- Shaving and washing hands each use approximately 1 gallon of water.
- Dishwashing (hand washing and rinsing) uses approximately 5 gallons of water. An automatic dishwasher short cycle uses approximately 7 gallons.
- A clothing washing machine short cycle with minimal water level uses approximately 27 gallons of water.
- On Earth 97.5 percent of the water is saltwater, unfit for human use.
- The majority of freshwater is beyond our reach, locked into polar snow and ice.
- Less than 1 percent of freshwater is usable, amounting to only 0.01 percent of Earth's total water.
- The recommended basic water requirement per person per day is 50 liters. But people can get by with about 30 liters: 5 liters for drinking and cooking and another 25 to maintain hygiene.
- By the mid-1990s, eighty countries, home to 40 percent of the world's population, encountered serious water shortages. The areas affected the most are Africa and the Middle East.
- Many women and young girls in sub-Saharan Africa must walk an estimated six miles every day to get enough water for their families.
- By 2025 two-thirds of the world's people will be facing water stress. The global demand for water will have grown by over 40 percent by then.

- Over 1 billion people, nearly 20 percent of the world's population, lack access to safe drinking water.
- In 2004, 2.2 million deaths worldwide were attributed to unsafe water; nine out of ten of these were children under five years of age.

The Basics of Sanitation

- One gram of feces can contain 10 million viruses, 1 million bacteria, 1 thousand parasite cysts, and a hundred worm eggs. Effective sanitation and hygiene are necessary to protect the water supply.
- Sanitation was voted "the greatest medical milestone in the last 150 years" in a poll for the *British Medical Journal.*
- Global statistics show that 2.4 billion people (40 percent of the world's population) entered the new millennium without access to hygienic sanitation facilities. About 1.9 billion of those without facilities were in Asia.
- Surveys show that the main reasons people want toilet facilities are for convenience, comfort, safety, and status—not sanitation.
- Ecosanitation processes, such as composting and urine diversion toilets, treat household waste as a resource for fertilizer and irrigation.
- The Millennium Development Goals (MDGs) urge governments to reduce by 50 percent the proportion of people who do not have sustainable access to safe drinking water and basic sanitation by the year 2015.
- From 1990 to 2002 the proportion of the population deemed to have access to adequate sanitation rose from 49 to 58 percent. That means an extra 87 million people gained access in that time period. To meet the MDG goal by 2015, that number must reach 75 percent.
- The World Health Organization (WHO) concluded that the $11.3 billion-a-year cost of halving the proportion of people without water and sanitation services would yield a benefit of $84 billion a year. Benefits take into account savings on health care, fewer work days lost to illness, and future earnings from averted deaths.

The Right to Water Movement

- The right to water means the fundamental human right of access to water of a quality, quantity, and accessibility sufficient to satisfy the basic human needs for drinking, hygiene, cleaning, cooking, subsistence agriculture for local food consumption, and sanitation.

- The right to water is explicitly enshrined in two UN (United Nations) human rights treaties. The UN Committee on Economic, Social, and Cultural Rights (CESCR) confirmed the right to water in its General Comment No. 15.
- The CESCR's General Comment No. 15 states that "Ensuring that everyone has access to adequate sanitation is not only fundamental for human dignity and privacy, but is one of the principal mechanisms for protecting the quality of drinking water supplies and resources."
- An international document guaranteeing that everyone has a right to safe and affordable water—a document that would be binding for national governments and that would provide a model and mechanism for the implementation of this right—does not exist.
- Green Cross International and its partners are proposing the negotiation and adoption of a framework convention on the right to water, which, when ratified by the member states of the United Nations, will give to all people a tool through which to assert their right to safe water and sanitation and would oblige national governments to make sure that this right is respected.
- The right to water does not mean that water is to be free of charge. However, individuals are entitled to water that is affordable.
- Water rights activists assert that water should be treated as a social and cultural good, a public good, and not primarily as an economic good; water cannot be treated as a commodity.

Simple Ways to Save Water
- Watering the lawn only when it needs it saves 750–1,500 gallons per month.
- Setting the lawn mower blade one inch higher means the grass needs less water, saving 500–1,500 gallons per month.
- Mulching around trees and plants saves 750–1,500 gallons per month.
- Xeriscaping, replacing the lawn and landscaping plants with drought-resistant plants, saves 750–1,500 gallons per month.
- Covering a swimming pool reduces evaporation and lessens the amount of water needed to refill the pool, saving 1,000 gallons per month.
- Fixing leaky plumbing saves 20 gallons per day per fixed leak.

- Washing the car with a bucket and quick hose rinse saves 150 gallons per wash.
- Installing water-saving showerheads saves 500–800 gallons per month.
- Running the dishwasher and clothes washer only when full saves 300–800 gallons per month.
- Shortening showers by one or two minutes saves 700 gallons per month.
- Using a broom instead of a hose to clean the driveway saves 150 gallons each time.
- Putting a plastic bottle filled with rocks in the toilet tank displaces some of the water, saving up to 300 gallons per month.
- Turning off the water while brushing teeth saves 3 gallons of water per day.
- Keeping a bottle of drinking water in the refrigerator, instead of running tap water until it is cool enough to drink, saves 200–300 gallons a month.
- Using the microwave to defrost foods instead of running water saves 50–150 gallons of water per month.
- Preventing children from playing with the garden hose saves 10 gallons per minute.
- Disposing of hazardous materials improperly pollutes the water supply. One quart of oil can contaminate 250,000 gallons of water.

Organizations to Contact

The editors have compiled the following list of organizations concerned with the issues debated in this book. The descriptions are derived from materials provided by the organizations. All have publications or information available for interested readers. The list was compiled on the date of publication of the present volume; the information provided here may change. Be aware that many organizations take several weeks or longer to respond to inquiries, so allow as much time as possible.

Environmental Protection Agency (EPA)
Ariel Rios Bldg.
1200 Pennsylvania Ave. NW
Washington, DC 20460
(202) 272-0167
TTY (speech- and hearing-impaired); (202) 272-0165
www.epa.gov

The EPA was established in 1970 by the White House and Congress in response to public outcry for cleaner water, air, and land. The EPA's mission is to protect human health and the environment. The educational resources section of the EPA's Web site includes water-related documents, research reports, and interactive learning tools.

Federal Emergency Management Agency (FEMA)
500 C St. SW
Washington, DC 20472
(800) 621-FEMA (3362)
fax: (800) 827-8112
e-mail: FEMA-Correspondence-Unit@dhs.gov
www.fema.gov

FEMA's primary mission is to reduce the loss of life and property and protect the nation from all hazards, including natural disasters, acts of terrorism, and other man-made disasters, by leading and supporting the nation in a risk-based, comprehensive emergency management system of preparedness, protection, response, recovery, and mitigation, To accomplish its mission, FEMA does a tremendous amount of research on water and dams and offers numerous documents to download from its Web site.

Global Water
3600 S. Harbor Blvd., # 514
Oxnard, CA 93035
(805) 985-3057
fax: (805) 985-3688
e-mail: info@globalwater.org
www.globalwater.org

Global Water is an international nonprofit, nongovernmental organization dedicated to helping to provide clean drinking water for developing countries. The organization provides technical assistance, water supply equipment, and volunteers to help poor countries develop safe and effective water supply programs around the world. Global Water's Web site offers a video titled *Dying of Thirst* and a slide show, *Live a Life That Matters.* The Web site also provides links and documents to download.

Intergovernmental Panel on Climate Change (IPCC)
IPCC Secretariat C/O World Meteorological Organization
7bis Ave. de la Paix, C.P. 2300, CH - 1211 Geneva 2, Switzerland
+41-22-730-8208
fax: +41-22-730-8025
e-mail: IPCC-Sec@wmo.int
www.ipcc.ch

The World Meteorological Organization (WMO) and the United Nations Environment Programme (UNEP) established the IPCC in 1988. The role of the IPCC is to assess information relevant to understanding the scientific basis of risk of human-induced climate change, its potential impacts, and options for adaptation and mitigation. The IPCC Web site is a rich resource for current press releases, global climate change reports, links, and publications.

International Water Management Institute (IWMI)
PO Box 2075, Colombo, Sri Lanka
+94-11 2787404, 2784080
fax: +94-11 2786854
e-mail: iwmi@cgiar.org
www.iwmi.cgiar.org

The IWMI is a nonprofit scientific organization funded by the Consultative Group on International Agricultural Research (CGIAR). IWMI concentrates on water and related land management challenges faced by poor rural communities. Its Web site offers maps, publications, research reports, and documents.

Louisiana Coastal Wetlands Conservation and Restoration Taskforce
Public Affairs Office, U.S. Army Corps of Engineers
PO Box 60267
New Orleans, LA 70160-0267
(504) 862-2201
e-mail: heidi-hitter@usgs.gov
www.lacoast.gov

The Louisiana Coastal Wetlands Conservation and Restoration Taskforce Web site is funded by the Coastal Wetlands Planning, Protection and Restoration Act (CWPPRA), which Congress passed in 1990. It funds wetland enhancement projects nationwide. This Web site contains general wetlands information, links, projects, *WaterMarks* magazine, educational materials, and other publications.

Natural Resources Defense Council (NRDC)
40 West 20th St.
New York, NY 10011
(212) 727-2700
fax: (212) 727-1773
e-mail: nrdcinfo@nrdc.org
www.nrdc.org

The NRDC is a U.S.-based environmental action organization that uses law, science, and the support of 1.2 million members and online activists to protect the planet's wildlife and wild places and to ensure a safe and healthy environment for all living things. Its Web site includes a section on clean water and oceans with numerous news items, reports, and links about drinking water, pollution, oceans, and conservation and restoration of water resources.

National Water Resources Association (NWRA)
3800 North Fairfax Dr., Suite 4
Arlington, VA 22203

(703) 524-1544
fax: (703) 524-1548
e-mail: nwra@nwra.org
www.nwra.org

The NWRA is a nonprofit federation of state organizations whose membership includes rural water districts, municipal water entities, commercial companies, and individuals. The NWRA is concerned with the appropriate management, conservation, and use of water and land resources in the United States. The Web site contains news releases, court cases, and links.

UNESCO World Water Assessment Programme
7 place de Fontenoy
75352 Paris 07 SP, France
+33 (0)1 45 68 10 00
fax: +33 (0)1 45 67 16 90
e-mail: waterportal@unesco.org
www.unesco.org/water/wwap

The World Water Assessment Programme is part of the United Nations Educational, Cultural, and Scientific Organization (UNESCO) and is designed to provide information related to global freshwater issues. Every three years it publishes the United Nations *World Water Development Report* (*WWDR*), a comprehensive review that gives an overall picture of the state of the world's freshwater resources and aims to provide decision-makers with the tools to implement sustainable use of our water. The *WWDR* is available for download, along with facts and figures, case studies, and other resources.

United Nations Development Programme (UNDP)
One United Nations Plaza
New York, NY 10017
(212) 906-5000
fax: (212) 906-5304
www.undp.org

UNDP is the United Nations' global development network, an organization advocating for change and connecting countries to knowledge, experience, and resources to help people build a better life. Water is a key issue, and the UNDP is a rich resource for documents such as *Beyond Scarcity: Power, Poverty, and the Global Water Crisis* and the *Millennium Development Goals* and other comprehensive documents, all available at its Web site.

U.S. Geological Survey (USGS)

USGS National Center
12201 Sunrise Valley Dr.
Reston, VA 20192
(888) 275-8747
http://water.usgs.gov

Water Resources is one of four science disciplines of the U.S. Geological Survey (USGS). Its mission is to provide reliable, impartial, timely information about U.S. water resources. The USGS Web site offers basic explanations and diagrams of water systems, issues, and management tools, as well as more complex reports and documents.

Water Partners International

2405 Grand Blvd.
860, Box 12
Kansas City, MO 64108
(913) 312-8600
www.water.org

WaterPartners International is a U.S.-based nonprofit organization committed exclusively to providing safe drinking water and sanitation to people in developing countries. The Web site offers a newsletter, research, *Ripples* magazine, brochures, and links.

Water Resources Research Center (WRRC)

University of Arizona
350 N. Campbell Ave.
Tucson, AZ 85721
(520) 792-9591, ext. 21
fax: (520) 792-8518
e-mail: smegdal@cals.arizona.edu
www.ag.arizona.edu/azwater

The WRRC promotes an understanding of water management issues through research and education. The WRRC is committed to assisting communities, educating teachers and students about water, and encouraging research. The WRRC offers a vast array of educational materials—some specific to the Southwest and Arizona and some more general in nature—at its Web site.

Water Supply and Sanitation Collaborative Council (WSSCC)
International Environment House
9 Chemin des Anémones
1219 Châtelaine, Geneva, Switzerland
+41 22 917 8657
fax: +41 22 917 8084
e-mail: wsscc@who.int
www.wsscc.org

The WSSCC exists under a mandate from the United Nations. The organization focuses exclusively on those people around the world who currently lack water and sanitation. The WSSCC Web site is a rich resource of publications, speeches, and documentation.

The World Bank
1818 H St. NW
Washington, DC 20433
(202) 473-1000
fax: (202) 477-6391
www.worldbank.org

The World Bank is an international organization that provides loans, grants, and technical assistance to developing countries around the world to help them reduce poverty and improve education, health, infrastructure, communications, and many other critical areas of national development. Its Web site contains news and information about global water issues under the heading Water Supply and Sanitation. This site includes numerous documents, research reports, and publications.

World Water Council (WWC)
Espace Gaymard, 2-4 place d'Arvieux
13002 Marseille, France
+33 4 91 99 41 00
fax: +33 4 9199 41 01
www.worldwatercouncil.org

The WWC was established in 1996 in response to increasing concern from the global community about world water issues. Its mission is to promote awareness, build political commitment, and trigger action on critical water issues at all levels to facilitate the efficient management and use of water on an environmentally sustainable basis. The WWC Web site includes a vast array of documents, research reports, new releases, case studies, and publications.

For Further Reading

Books

Clark, Arthur P., Muhammad A. Tahlawi, William Facey, and Thomas A. Pledge. *A Land Transformed: The Arabian Peninsula, Saudi Arabia, and Saudi Aramco.* Dhahran, Saudi Arabia: Saudi Arabian Oil Co. (Saudi Aramco); Houston, TX: Aramco Services Co., 2006. A historical overview of how oil has changed the landscape in the Middle East and the impact it had on ancient and current water sources.

Conkin, Paul Keith. *The State of the Earth: Environmental Challenges on the Road to 2100.* Lexington: University Press of Kentucky, 2007. A passionate plea to admit man's negative impact on the soil and water and to make changes to protect the planet.

Grossman, Elizabeth. *Watershed: The Undamming of America.* New York: Counterpoint, 2002. A celebration of undammed, free-flowing rivers and a survey of why communities are considering this option.

Grunwald, Michael. *The Swamp: The Everglades, Florida, and the Politics of Paradise.* New York: Simon & Schuster, 2006. Written by the winner of the 2003 Society of Environmental Journalists Award, this book tells the compelling story of how politics ruined and then reclaimed the Florida wetlands.

Hunt, Constance Elizabeth. *Thirsty Planet: Strategies for Sustainable Water Management.* London: Zed, 2004. This book sets out to prove that instead of dividing the water between nature and humans, the only real hope is to give absolute priority to water conservation.

Lancaster, Brad. *Rainwater Harvesting for Drylands and Beyond.* Vol. 1, *Guiding Principles to Welcome Rain into Your Life and Landscape.* Tucson, AZ: Brad Lancaster, 2006. This award-winning, self-published book shows people how to harvest the rainwater in their own backyard.

Leslie, Jacques. *Deep Water: The Epic Struggle over Dams, Displaced People, and the Environment.* New York: Farrar, Straus, and Giroux, 2005. A global look at dams and the unintentional and disheartening impact they have had in India, Africa, and Australia.

McDonald, David A., and Greg Ruiters. *The Age of Commodity: Water Privatization in Southern Africa.* London: Earthscan, 2005. A comprehensive look at the paradoxes and debates of "free water" and "water for sale" in Southern Africa.

Midkiff, Kenneth. *Not a Drop to Drink: America's Water Crisis (and What You Can Do).* Novato, CA: New World Library, 2007. Written by one of America's leading experts on water, this book takes readers straight to the source—water managers who run ranches and communities—and imparts practical answers for complex water problems.

Morris, Robert D. *The Blue Death: Disease, Disaster, and the Water We Drink.* New York: HarperCollins, 2007. A water epidemiologist, this author warns that climate change, toxic chemicals, and decaying municipal pipes are all threatening the water that is piped right into America's kitchen sinks.

Neilsen, Ron. *The Little Green Handbook: Seven Trends Shaping the Future of Our Planet.* New York: Picador, 2006. A definitive guide to twenty-first century environmental challenges—including water resource management—with the goal of ensuring a sustainable future for the next generation.

Patton, Kimberley C. *The Sea Can Wash Away All Evils: Modern Marine Pollution and the Ancient Cathartic Ocean.* New York: Columbia University Press, 2007. A powerful reminder that ethics, morality, and religious perspective all influence the way the global community solves the global water crisis.

Pearce, Fred. *When the Rivers Run Dry: Water, the Defining Crisis of the Twenty-first Century,* Boston: Beacon Press, 2006. Former *New Scientist* news editor Fred Pearce examines the crisis of wells, wetlands, and rivers around the world.

Roddick, Anita. *Troubled Waters: Saints, Sinners, Truth and Lies About the Global Water Crisis.* Chichester, UK, Anita Roddick Books, 2004. An exposé of current water politics that have millions of poor people dying for a drink of water while millions of citizens in industrial nations pay outrageous prices for designer water and even buy beef-flavored water for their dogs.

Segerfeldt, Fredrik. *Water for Sale: How Business and the Market Can Resolve the World's Water Crisis.* Washington, DC: Cato Institute,

2005. A vote for privatization, this book uses case studies to demonstrate that privatization is getting water to people who were previously ignored and to show that claims by the antiprivatization lobby are largely unfounded.

Thomas, Duncan A., and Roger R. Ford. *The Crisis of Innovation in Water and Wastewater.* Cheltenham, UK: Edward Elgar, 2005. A comprehensive investigation of how technology and holistic policy can work together to create a sustainable solution to the water and sewer management crisis.

Periodicals

Ball, Julie. "Storm Water Runoff Erodes Some Buncombe Hillsides," *Ashville Citizen-Times,* January 22, 2006.

Bergeron, Angelle. "System Failure Gets Blame in New Orleans," *Engineering News-Record,* June 12, 2006.

Blevins, Jason, and Charlie Meyers. "A River Untamed," *Denver Post,* July 10, 2007.

Bowen, Shannan. "Counties Put Water on Front Burner," *Star News,* July 31, 2007.

Breitler, Alex. "Officials Worry over San Francisco Possibly Siphoning Off Water Supply," *Record,* July 29, 2007.

Chang, Gordon G. "Beijing's Dilemma," *Wall Street Journal,* March 31, 2007.

Crowder, Larry. "The Oceans Need a Hand: There's Only One Way to Save the Seas," *Los Angeles Times,* August 6, 2006.

Downing, Bob. "Ohio EPA Wades into Troubled Creek," *Akron Beacon Journal,* August 19, 2007.

Harlow, Tim. "Chanhassen Slaps Ban on Irrigation Systems, Sprinklers," *Star Tribune,* July 25, 2007.

Jackon, Bill. "Riesberg Water Forum Reinforces Complex Water Issues," *Greeley Tribune,* August 17, 2007.

Kruger, Harold. "State Promises Dam Benefits," *Appeal-Democrat,* April 14, 2006.

Kuhles, Beth. "County Looks at New Water Resources," *Houston Chronicle,* July 20, 2006.

Lowy, Joan. "New Angles on the Environment," *CQ Weekly*, April 18, 2005.

Mackin, Kerry. "Time to Stop Gambling with Our Water Future," *Boston Globe*, September 15, 2005.

Mann, Charles C. "The Rise of Big Water," *Vanity Fair*, May 2007.

Marks, Jane C. "Down Go the Dams," *Scientific American*, March 2007.

Matlock, Staci. "Farmer's Water Fight Still Not Resolved," *Santa Fe New Mexican*, August 13, 2007.

McClenahen, John S. "Waste Not Want Not," *Industry Week*, February 1, 2007.

Norris, Michelle. "Drought Complicates Water Works in Montana," *All Things Considered* (NPR), August 7, 2007.

Okonski, K., and C. Boin. "Free Water from State Control," *Economic Times*, September 26, 2007.

Park, Sid. "Three Gorges Dam Is Affecting Ocean Life," *Science News*, May 20, 2006.

Risbud, Aditi. "Cheap Drinking Water from the Ocean," *Technology Review*, June 12, 2006.

Rosen, Rick. "Consider an Irrigation System That Saves Water, Money," *Dallas Morning News*, August 9, 2007.

Rucker, Phillip. "System Would Use Effluent to Produce Power," *Washington Post*, August 19, 2007.

Shnayerson, Michael. "A Convenient Truth," *Vanity Fair*, May 2007.

Thigpen, Daniel. "Lodi Sewage Disposal May Be Affecting Groundwater," *Record*, August 18, 2007.

Waggoner, John. "Investors Fish for Profit in Clean Water," *USA Today*, May 23, 2007.

Will, George F. "Arizona's Thirst for Ingenuity," *Washington Post*, April 23, 2006.

Index

Picture Credits

Maury Aaseng, 13, 23, 28, 36, 40, 48, 57, 64, 70, 74, 81, 93, 97, 104, 111, 120, 125, 135

AP Images, 10, 21, 30, 34, 43, 51, 55, 61, 68, 75, 79, 85, 92, 98, 100, 103, 114, 118, 127, 133

Cartoon by Ed Fischer. Www.CartoonStock.com, 89

© 2007 Jennifer Greve, 16

Piero Pomponi/Liaison/Getty Images, 47